Arthur Keats.

Compliments of J. B. Leander.

THE

ARGONAUTS OF 'FORTY-NINE

SOME RECOLLECTIONS OF THE PLAINS AND THE DIGGINGS

BY

DAVID ROHRER LEEPER

ILLUSTRATED

By O. Marion Elbel, from Seleotions and Suggestions

by the Author

"Golden days, remembered days,
The days of 'Forty-Nine"

SOUTH BEND, INDIANA
J. B. STOLL & COMPANY, PRINTERS
1894

Copyright, 1894 and 1895,

BY DAVID ROHRER LEEPER.

All rights reserved.

THE ARGONAUTS OF ,'FORTY-NINE.

I.

HO, FOR THE SACRAMENTO!

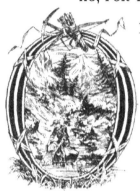 N FEBRUARY 22, 1849, our little party of six set out from South Bend, Indiana, for the newly discovered gold-fields of California. The members of this party were William S. Good, Michael Donahue, Thomas Rockhill, William L. Earl, Thomas Dudley Neal, and the writer (David R. Leeper). All were young — the oldest twenty-five, the youngest seventeen. Our equipment consisted of two wagons, seven yoke of oxen, and two years' supplies. The long journey before us, the comparatively unknown region through which it lay, and the glamour of the object for which it was undertaken, lent our adventure considerable local interest, so that many friends and spectators were present to witness our departure, our two covered wagons being objects of much curious concern as they rolled out Washington street, with their three thousand miles chiefly of wilderness before them. But for us the occasion had few pangs. The diggings had been discovered but a twelvemonth before, and the glowing tales of their marvellous rich-

ness were on every tongue. Our enthusiasm was
wrought up to the highest pitch, while the hardships
and perils likely to be incident to such a journey were
given scarcely a passing thought. Several parties of
our acquaintance had already gone, and others were
preparing to go, which still further intensified our
eagerness. It was therefore with light hearts, and perhaps lighter heads, that we lustily joined in the chorus
of the inspiring parody of the time:

"Oh, California!
That's the land for me;
I'm going to Sacramento
With my washbowl on my knee."

The West was still very new. Even Chicago had
not heard the whistle of the locomotive. Illinois,
Iowa and Missouri were, for the most part, an un-
broken prairie expanse, with not infrequently ten to
twenty miles between the nearest settlers. The coo-
ing of myriads of prairie chickens filled the morning
air like the roar of a distant waterfall, and the prairies
were strewn over with the antlers of the deer and elk,
attesting the abundance also of this more pretentious
species of game. Westward of Iowa and Missouri,
that vast area of mountain and plain stretching away
to where the surf-beat of the Pacific laves the golden
shore, was laid down on the maps as terra incognita.
Except at three or four isolated spots, where a mission or a military post had been located, not an abode
of the white man was to be seen from the Missouri
River to the Sacramento. True, the Later Day
Saints, wandering about in search of the Holy Land,
like the Israelites of old, had dropped down by the
Great Salt Lake two years before, but the bulk of

SCENE ON THE CALIFORNIA EMIGRANT ROAD.

gold-seekers went on other roads, and were therefore not permitted to feast eyes on the few mud huts that then adorned this newly adopted land of promise.

We were not long in finding out that the adventure meant something more than poetry and romance. We left home in the midst of a thaw, and from the very start were beset with the mud, slush and flood incident to the breaking up of winter. Especially upon the murky prairies, of which we saw little else till we reached the frontier, the roads were wretched in the extreme. Several of the parties from South Bend drove their teams only as far as the Mississippi River, where, wearied of their tedious progress, they shipped their wagons and goods by boat to their intended point of departure on the frontier, driving their teams thence' loose across the country. Our party, however, braved it through overland from beginning to end. Nor did we indeed have much choice in the matter, for it so happened that we were out from home but a few days when all the hard cash in our company's exchequer mysteriously took wing. We were frequently compelled to make wide detours, avoiding the roads altogether, so as to escape the floods and bottomless lowlands. Many of the streams were out of their banks, and the bridges (if there had been any) were washed away. At LaSalle, Illinois, we were water-bound for a week or more by the swollen Little Vermillion Creek. We made an effort to cross by swimming a yoke of oxen over and attaching a line from them to á wagon on the opposite bank. The wagon made the passage well enough;

but it had not occurred to us to lash down the box, and the vehicle had scarcely reached the current when

WILLIAM S. GOOD.
(FROM A DAGUERREOTYPE, 1852.)

the box lifted from its place, and dashed away on the foaming torrent as gaily as if on a holiday jaunt. Luckily, the jolly craft lodged at the aqueduct of the canal several miles below, and was thus prevented from being lost in the Illinois River, which was rushing by at flood-stage. Our goods had been removed from the box before we made the experiment. We finally, as a last resort, were compelled to swim our oxen across, drag our wagons through the aqueduct, and carry our luggage over on the heel-path, the toe-path being on the opposite side. At Burlington, Iowa, we had a similar detention. The bottoms of the Mississippi were inundated for miles, and ferriage for a time was wholly suspended. When finally, we were enabled to make the pas-

WILLIAM L. EARL.
(FROM AN OLD PHOTOGRAPH.)

sage, it was on board a rickety scow propelled by a horse treadmill, the distance between the landings on the opposite sides being seven miles. The current was against us at that, but a tortuous slough through a timbered bottom very much facilitated our progress. Added to the difficulties of travel, were the inconveniences suffered from the scantiness of accommodations for ourselves and animals incident to the newness and sparseness of the settlements. More than once we could obtain no accommodations at all. I remember that on one such occasion in Missouri, when after trudging all day long through the mud, night overtook us in the middle of a wide prairie. We had no alternative but to chain our oxen to the wheels of our wagons, make our couches beneath the wagon covers as best we could, having no fire and no food for man or beast. As I lay upon that rude pallet reflecting on the situation, the winds meantime keeping up an ominous refrain without, my thoughts naturally turned toward home, its blazing chimney-fire, its generous cupboard, and its other creature comforts. Only on one other occasion was I touched with homesickness during my five years' absence on that adventure. That was on receipt of my first letter from home, after an absence of two and a half years. We fared decidedly better after we had left all traces of civilization behind. Then the roads were easier; we carried our own food; and our animals subsisted on the native pastures.

But the irksomeness of this part of the journey was somewhat relieved by the naturally buoyant proclivities of most of the party. A little beyond Joliet, Illinois, our numbers were augmented by a party of South Benders about the size of ours. Thus recruited, we

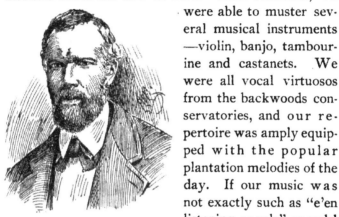

THOMAS ROCKHILL.
(FROM A PHOTOGRAPH, 1881.)

were able to muster several musical instruments —violin, banjo, tambourine and castanets. We were all vocal virtuosos from the backwoods conservatories, and our repertoire was amply equipped with the popular plantation melodies of the day. If our music was not exactly such as "e'en listening angels" would "lean to hear," we were nevertheless enabled in this manner to while away many an evening by our camp-fires, which otherwise would have dragged heavily on our hands. In fact, our musical prepossessions were so pronounced that our fame spread far and near along our route, and won us the reputation of being the wildest and jolliest lot of Hoosiers ever let loose outside the hoop-pole and pumpkin state. Out on the plains, too, there was

DAVID R. LEEPER.
(FROM A PHOTOGRAPH, 1891.)

plenty of company. We were scarcely ever out of sight of other emigrants like ourselves, and our camps were often great villages, which were generally enlivened with music and dancing or some other sorts of amusements.

It must be owned, however, that camp experience was by no means conducive to exuberance of spirit or sweetness of temper. In fact, it was a matter of common remark that men were decidedly more irascible on the plains than they had been at home, and this perverseness not infrequently culminated in hot words and sometimes in blows. The tilts thus occasioned were made the theme of many comic songs out on the plains. Our first experience of the kind occurred at our encampment on the Mississippi, where we were awaiting ferriage. On this occasion, the chef de cuisine then on duty, had arranged a convenient seat for himself when preparing the meal, and it was noticed that he had not been altogether self-abnegating in apportioning the dried-apple sauce among the several plates. He had, in fact, served the delicacy in decidedly less stinted measure to himself than to the others. One of the other members of the mess, observing this, did not propose to brook the offense, and with words, looks and gestures betokening blows brushed the offender aside and seated himself at the favored plate. Trifling as this affair was, the participants were never friends afterward.

Good and Earl sported better clothes than their companions. On starting upon the journey, the one wore a silk hat and the other a swallowtail coat. The

GOLD MINING WITH ROCKER AND LONG-TOM IN 'FORTY-NINE.

hat soon became badly battered, and at the mid-prai-
rie encampment, mentioned on another page, one of the
sleeves of the coat worked down between the wagon
cover and the wagon box within reach of the oxen
chained to the wheel and was chewed into pulp up to
the elbow.   Earl, well knowing how his companions
relished the mishap, continued out of spite to wear the
garment as before.   At one of our encampments
shortly after, one of our many visitors from the neighborhood was a rustic who was soon to be married,
He was readily persuaded that the hat and coat could
be made to answer for a part of his wedding suit.

For a trifle, he was told,
he could have the articles
restored as good as new in
St. Joseph, which was some
thirty to forty miles distant.
An exchange for a good
rifle was quickly consum-
mated.   The weapon was
thought to be a valuable ac-
quisition, for mine had disappeared early on the jour-

JUST THE THING.

ney, and we felt that surely we must be armed to the
teeth after crossing the border.

St. Joseph, Missouri, was our objective point on the
frontier.   We found this border city—the last outpost
of civilization—thronged with gold-seekers like ourselves.   They had flocked hither from every quarter
to fit out for the overland journey.   Many had pushed
out before our arrival; many were still coming in; and

all was hurry-scurry with excitement. The only transportation available for crossing the Missouri River
was a big clumsy scow or flat-boat propelled by long
oars or sweeps. We chartered this craft for one night,
several parties clubbing with us for the purpose. The
price stipulated was ninety dollars, we to perform the
labor. The task was by no means a holiday diversion. I tugged at the end of one of those sweeps myself all night, and it seemed a long, long night, indeed.
'The Big Muddy was booming from the spring freshets, and at this point hurled its entire volume sheer
against a precipitous bluff just above the ferrying-
place, thus lashing its waters, ordinarily very violent,
into redoubled fury. But we were equal to the emergency, and succeeded in placing the turbulent flood
behind not only ourselves, but also enough others fully to idemnify us for our outlay.

On May 16, we pulled out from the Missouri River
through the muddy timbered bottom to the open bluffs.
We had now, sure enough, bid adieu to civilization.
The wild beast and the sportive, hair-lifting savage
rose up in grim visions before us, as the fancy painted
forth the haunts of the cheerless solitude. Over two
thousand miles of this sort of forbidding prospect lay
before us. A strong force and a rigid discipline were
very naturally conceived of as the imperative needs of
the hour. Many emigrants—as we were all denomi-
nated at that time—were encamped about us, and all
were impressed with a like portentous sense of the situation. We were, therefore, not long in marshaling
a train of some sixty wagons, duly equipped with of-

ficers and a bristling code of rules.   Guards were to
pace their beats regularly of nights, and the stock was
all to be carefully corralled by arranging the wagons
in the form of an enclosure for this purpose.   Johnson
Horrell, who was for many years a conspicuous figure
in the history of South Bend, was given the chief command.   As we pushed out from the river bluffs into
the open country beyond, our long line of "prairie
schooners" looked sightly indeed, as it gracefully
wound itself over the green, billowy landscape,

"Stretching in airy undulations far away."

But, as we soon found out, our "thing of beauty"
was not to be "a joy forever."   It was ordered, among
other regulations, that the teams retain permanently
the order in which they had fallen into line on the
first day, only that the procession should be operated
as a sort of endless chain, each team in its turn occupying the lead one day and dropping to the rear the
next day.   Nothing could appear fairer or more im-
partial than this arrangement.   Yet, the spirit of re-
volt was alive and imminent.   The driver—James
McCartney, a resolute South Bender—who enjoyed
the post of honor on the first day, insisted on retaining
the same position on the next day, and he did, in spite
of all expostulations and peremptory commands to the
contrary.   A court martial was ordered; but the re-
calcitrant was inexorable.   He simply scouted the authority of that grave tribunal, and thereafter drove
and encamped at a convenient distance from the main
body, thus largely profiting by the supposed advan-

tages of the organization, while wholly relieved of its duties and inconveniences.

I may here relate a trifling incident illustrative of a conspicuous feature of the plains that season. We had not been out many days beyond the confines of civilization, when, in a stroll some distance from the train, I discovered a good wagon tire. Such reckless abandonment of property was something new to me. I rolled the valuable article along for a while, striving vigorously to reach the moving train with it, but had at last to abandon the effort in despair. From about this time onward, we saw castaway articles strewn by the roadside one after another in increasing profusion till we could have taken our choice of the best of wagons entire with much of their lading, had we been provided with the extra teams to draw them. Some of the draft animals perished, some stampeded, and all became more or less jaded and foot-worn. One train, from Columbus, Ohio, lost every animal it had through that inexplicable fright known as stampede. Hence the means for transportation became inadequate thus early on the journey, and were every day becoming more and more reduced. Many of the emigrants had provided enough supplies to last them a year or two; but they were not long in seeing the pro-

EVENING CAMP SCENE ON THE PLATTE—FLIPPING FLAPJACKS.

priety, if not the actual necessity, of reducing their lading as much as possible, with the view both of relieving their teams and facilitating their progress. Even the wagon boxes were in many cases shortened, and tons upon tons of bacon and other articles of the outfits were converted into fuel, the main purpose being to favor the teams.

Fuel was quite an object through that part of the route now known as Nebraska and Eastern Wyoming. On the lower part of the main Platte, the situation as to wood was somewhat like that described in the Grecian fable as to water: ·

> "So bends tormented Tantalus to drink,
> While from his lips the refluent waters shrink;
> Again the rising stream his bosom laves,
> And thirst consumes him 'mid circumfluent waves."

For a number of days, a heavy belt of cottonwoods was temptingly near at hand; but not in a single instance were we able to reach a trunk, limb, or twig because of an intervening section of the river. Weeds and buffalo "chips" (*bois de vache*) were about our only resource, and the latter, I may say, made an excellent fuel when it could be had. To husband as much as possible the scanty supply of such fuel as was obtainable, we improvised a sort of furnace by cutting a narrow trench in the sod so that the coffee-pot and frying-pan would span the breadth of the fire and rest upon the walls of the opening. Coffee, flapjacks and bacon were about the only articles we had to prepare, and in the turning or "flipping" of the flapjacks, especially, we soon became very expert.

As to our grand caravan, it steadily came to grief. The inexpediency of traveling in so large a body be-

came more and more manifest as we approached the
mountains, and the rough roads and difficult passages
delayed progress by the necessity of one team having
to wait on another, especially where the doubling of
teams was required.   Other influences tended to the
same end.   As we became accustomed to the plains,
our wariness from visions of the tomahawk and the
scalping-knife gradually wore away into stolid indifference, so that we cared nothing for the security that
numbers might afford.   I carried no arms, yet often
wandered miles away from the train alone as this or
that object might happen to attract my attention.
The parching winds and stifling dust, with the boun-
tifully blotched and blistered lips that afflicted nearly
every one in consequence, did not at all conduce to
that geniality of temper that would incline men to social solace.   Besides, on the earlier part of the route,
there was much sickness, and many deaths occurred,
which occasioned annoyances and delays irksome to
those not immediately interested.   It is not very
strange, therefore, that, with all these dismembering
tendencies at work, our once imposing pageant should
have so ingloriously faded that before we had fairly
reached the mountains it had passed into "innocuous
desuetude."   Even our own little party underwent
depletions from time to time until but three members
of the original six remained.   These three traveled
and camped alone for many days, with the utmost unconcern as to whether anybody else was far or near.
As for keeping watch, all thought of that had vanish-
ed before we had proceeded a quarter of our way,

Tents, too, were early abandoned as useless luxuries, and each individual when retiring for the night, sought out the most eligible site he could find (usually among the sage-brush), and rolling himself up in his blankets and buffalo robes thus committed himself to the "sweet restorer," with only the starry canopy for a shelter;—[1]

"Weariness
Can snore upon the flint, when rusty sloth
Finds the downy pillow hard."

In connection with the matter of guard duty, a little digression here in the way of a personal allusion may be excusable. The occurrence happened while some pretense of numbers and military formalities was still affected. My guard-shift came on at midnight. It was alleged that I failed to respond to the call of the sentinel whom I was to relieve. It was at the time raining and blustering forbiddingly without. It was much more inviting beneath the protecting wagon sheets than out upon the bleak, howling plain. Hence the presumption of guilt lay manifestly against me, and I was promptly arraigned and tried on the charge. A witty and brilliant attorney from Columbus, Ohio, volunteered to defend me. The counsel laid much stress on my unsophisticated make-up, and thus in a serio-comic vein affected to appeal to the sympathy of the court. But the court nevertheless remained inexorable, and a double stent of guard duty was the finding. Whether or not that judgment was ever carried into effect, is a matter that does not appear of record.

Near where we forded the South Platte we had the

---

1 See "Moonlight camp scene on the Humboldt," on page 52.

A SIOUX VILLAGE. (AFTER A SKETCH BY GEORGE CATLIN.)

good fortune to come upon a large village of the Sioux which was squatted temporarily in the locality. These Indians struck me as being decidedly comely specimens of their race—neat, healthy, self-poised. Their dress was made chiefly of white-tanned skins, and looked very picturesque in its elaborate decorations of beadwork and other fanciful adornments peculiar to savagery. I had the honor of being one of a party that called upon the chief in his tepee, and of exchanging whiffs of the pipe of peace with that "much heap big Ingin." Our dignified host at once bespoke our confidence by his gracious assurance that the Sioux had never shed the blood of the pale-face. During the whole of the ceremony, one of the attaches of his royal muckamuck regaled us with a half-gutteral, half-nasal chant, to which he marked time with the swing of the rattle.

Game was by no means as plentiful as one would have supposed. We found more of it in the states through which we passed than in the country beyond. In the region now known as Nebraska many antelopes were seen bounding over the plain or watching our movements from elevated points; but they were shy, vigilant, and hard to capture. In the mountains, deer and mountain sheep (*ovis montana*) were occasionally sighted and brought down, and when we struck the magnificent pasture ranges of California, deer, elk, antelope and bear abounded. At the "Big Meadows," on Feather River, where we lay by several days to recruit our oxen, Neal brought in seven black-tail deer in one day. I was out at the same time

"A SPIRITED CHASE."

equally eager on the chase, but the game did not appear at all enamored of my presence, so I had my am-
munition for my pains.   But, on the whole, our banquets on the luxuries of the chase were few and far
between.   Strange to say, we saw but few buffaloes
(properly bison), not more than a dozen or so, all told.
Those few we saw near where we forded the South
Platte.[1]   A spirited chase was being given the tempt-
ing stragglers, and this within plain view of our moving caravan.   The spectacle was rendered none the
less inspiring from the circumstance that a lady mounted on a fleet steed was one of the party making the
pursuit.

1 The writer was privileged, nearly thirty years later, when steaming
down the Missouri River through the Bad Lands, to witness those noble
beasts in their wonted glory.   It was in August, and they were on their
northward run.   The steamer was several days in passing through their scattered bands, groups of which were well-nigh constantly in sight   Several
times the boat ran over clumps of them, as they were, swimming the river.
At one point we came upon perhaps thirty to forty of them where they were
confined on a narrow sand spit between the river and a high vertical bluff.
The frightened animals took to the water, and a part of them became mired
in a mud bank on the opposite side, where the captain ran the steamer upon
them and sixteen were wantonly slaughtered.   Squads of the passengers kept
up a constant fusilade among the poor brutes from the hurricane deck, as the
steamer was passing through their lines, killing and maiming many—all, too,
with rifles and ammunition furnished the boat by the Government for defense against hostile Indians.

II.

A CHANGE OF SCENE—THE ARID REGION.

W E forded the South Fork of the Platte. It was, at our place of crossing, a broad, shallow stream, with a treacherous quicksand bottom. The accompanying cut presents a typical scene of the fording. From this branch of the Platte, our trail lay over a high, open, rolling country, via Ash Hollow, for a distance of about fifty miles, to the North Fork of the Platte. We then followed the course of the latter stream some three hundred miles. The country now gradually increased in ruggedness, thus heralding our approach toward the Rocky Mountains. The cliffs and highlands along the Platte became objects of special interest. These cliffs, being composed of horizontal strata of different degrees of hardness, were in many instances wrought into various forms which, with a little assistance of the imagination, appeared to be artistic creations, such as churches, castles, towers, embattlements, and architectural ruins of various sorts. As Washington Irving remarks, one could scarcely persuade himself that works of art were not here really mingled with the fantastic freaks of nature.

We had now, very evidently, entered upon a land different from any to which we had ever before been

FORDING THE SOUTH PLATTE. (REDRAWN BY PERMISSION FROM "PACIFIC TOURIST." ADAMS & BISHOP, PUBLISHERS, NEW YORK.)

accustomed. The presence of the cacti and other arid-loving plants assured us that we were treading the soil of the so-called Arid Region, which comprises a third of the entire country. The villages of the prairie dog had become numerous, and the queer antics of this shy, vigilant, nimble, barking marmot afforded us much amusement. The stately owl and the lazy rattlesnake were the constant but doubtless unwelcome co-partners with the prairie dog in the occupancy of these villages.

The Court House Rock and the Chimney Rock[1] were among the more conspicuous of these natural curiosities, and both were visible a considerable distance. We took our nooning nearly opposite the first-

THE CHIMNEY ROCK.

named, which arose before us isolated and in bold relief out of the bosom of the plain. Ahead, in the direction we were going, the spire of the other was peeping invitingly over the intervening hills. It would be easy enough, to all appearances, to step over to the Court House, cut across to the Chimney, and reach the train by camping time. A party of us according-

1 I thus described this noted landmark in 1 64, when I last saw it: "It has a vertical column about seventy feet high, standing upon the apex of a conical base of about the same height and about a half mile in its largest circumference. A few years ago the lightning hurled some thirty feet of the chimney or spire to the ground, and the winds and the rains are slowly wearing away the remainder. The mass is evidently a detached section of the adjacent bluffs, and has been configured by the same processes of erosion as the formations of which it was once a part."

A PRAIRIE DOG VILLAGE.

ly determined upon the undertaking. We were all afoot, but the distance appeared so trifling as to give us no concern. Well, the upshot of it was, that we did not reach the Court House until about sundown. We hurriedly carved our names upon its walls; view ed for a moment the strange landscape roundabout; gazed down upon the crystal waters of a generous brook that rippled at its base, and, giving the Chimney an askance glance, were glad to bear away for camp, which we did not make till far in the night. It required still two and a half days journeying before we stood under the shadow of the Chimney. The extreme transparency of the atmosphere in this section explains the illusory phenomenon. Objects appeared but a mile or two away when in reality they were often from five to ten. Even the stars seemed to steal down from their wonted depths, and look vastly nearer, greater and grander as they set their vigils over us for the night. Little wonder, therefore, that such illusions should have taken the tenderfoot unawares, and more than once set him will-o'-the-wisp chasing.

About fifteen miles above Chimney Rock are Scott's Bluffs.[1] The high, picturesque escarpments which had been occupying our attention for several days here fell abruptly into the Platte, necessitating a circuit of some thirty miles across the uplands. A cut in the face of the cliffs about the width of a common wagon road and with perpendicular walls at the entrance three

---

1 Irving, in his "Captain Bonneville," relates a very pathetic story of one Scott in connection with these bluffs. A number of years prior to the period in which he was writing (1832), Scott had been taken ill and was abandoned by his companions on the Laramie River: "On the ensuing summer these very individuals visiting these parts, in company with others, came suddenly upon

to four hundred feet high, furnished a natural and easy
ascent.   Near the summit were an excellent spring
and an inviting camping ground.   A blacksmith had
here erected a temporary shop and was for the time
industriously plying his trade.   Even this rude makeshift of a habitation had a refreshing effect upon our
spirits, as a reminder of the civilization we had left far
behind.   The bluffs, as we first sighted them, treated
us to a magnificent optical illusion — a striking instance of the mirage.   The Platte seemed to be lifted
high from its bed and swollen into a mighty flood

SCOTT'S BLUFFS.—(REDRAWN BY
PERMISSION FROM "THE CEN-
TURY" FOR JULY, 1891.)

sweeping the entire val-
ley.   Out of this apparent expanse of rushing waters
the rugged form of the bluffs loomed up in blunted,

the bleached bones and grinning skull of a human skeleton, which, by certain
signs, they recognized for the remains of Scott. This was sixty long miles
from the place where they had abandoned him; and it appeared that the
wretched man had crawled that immense distance before death put an end to
his miseries. The wild and picturesque bluffs in the neighborhood of his lonely
grave have ever since borne his name."

blurred and exaggerated outline, a hazy, dreamy, tremulous atmosphere the while lending its weird-like effect to the scene.

We now began to catch an occasional glimpse of the outer and higher peaks of the Rocky Mountains. Laramie's Peak was the first of these to greet us.[1] In a few days more we passed Fort Laramie, where we entered the Black Hills, so called from the dark appearance at a distance of the scrubby cedars covering

LARAMIE'S PEAK.—REDRAWN BY PERMISSION FROM "THE CENTURY" FOR MARCH. 1891.)

the region. The road had become rougher and the soil more parched; but the change was hailed as a welcome relief from the long-continued monotony. We had actually grown weary of good roads, and sighed for something to shake us up. Another wel-

1 This peak was the first mountain that any of our immediate party had ever seen, and its proportions appeared to us very formidable.

come change was the abundance of fuel, and the numerous mountain streams of pure cold water. We here made our first acquaintance with the artemisia or sagebrush, which was thenceforward to be our chief reliance for fuel.[1]

The North Fork of the Platte, from which on leaving Fort Laramie we had made a detour of eighty miles, we crossed on a craft constructed of cottonwood dug-outs pinned together, which was purchased and sold by those who in turn used it. One of our wagons was swamped on being run aboard the contrivance, but the lading being chiefly flour little damage was done.

At the Red Buttes, we took final leave of the Platte, which had so long borne us company. It was still a considerable stream, being several hundred yards wide, with a deep and rapid current. An enterprising Mormon had located a current ferry-boat at this point, which proved a very profitable investment. Two days more took us to the Sweetwater, a clear, rapid tributary of the Platte, four feet deep and twenty yards wide. We were now upon the immediate confines of the Rocky Mountains proper. From the appearance of the specimens before us, the name "Rocky" seemed to have been readily enough suggested, for the entire mass in sight was of primitive rock wholly bare, and destitute of vegetation except here and there where a friendly crevice or indentation yielded a scanty and precarious sustenance to a few stunted trees or

1 This shrub occasionally grows six to eight feet in height, but generally only from one to two feet. It emits, especially when crushed, a strong wormwood odor, which from its almost constant presence became very obnoxious.

INDEPENDENCE ROCK. (REDRAWN BY PERMISSION FROM "PACIFIC TOURIST." ADAMS & BISHOP, PUBLISHERS, NEW YORK.)

THE BIG-HORN AT HOME.—ADAPTED BY PERMISSION FROM ROOSEVELT'S "THE HUNTING TRIPS OF A RANCHMAN," G. P. PUTNAM'S SONS, PUBLISHERS, NEW YORK AND LONDON,

shrubs. The signs of disintegration, too, were on all sides strikingly manifest. The huge bodies in place were rent into fragments from base to summit, and were ground off and furrowed out as only Nature's agencies could have fashioned them during long geologic time. The immense blocks, some of them acres in extent, had apparently been wrenched from the original ledges and strewn roundabout, as if some maddened Titan had been attempting to tear up the foundations of the earth and fling the fragments to the winds;—

> "The green earth shuddered, and shrank, and paled;
> The wave sprang up and the mountain quailed.
> Look on the hills; let the scars they bear
> Measure the pain of that hour's despair."

Independence Rock is the most noted of these detached landmarks. Standing immediately by the roadside as a sort of sentinel to the mountain flank, it was the first of these interesting objects to arrest our attention. Recent measurements make it one thousand five hundred and fifty yards in circumference and one hundred and ninety-three feet in height. Its side bordering the road was literally covered with names and dates; as, according to Fremont, it was when he first saw it, in 1842. We here celebrated the Fourth of July. The young lawyer who earlier had so gallantly defended me for sleeping on guard made the oration. The rock took its name from a similar celebration that took place there years before. We used the river water for camp purposes during our stop-over for the patriotic exercises. Imagine our chagrin and disgust when soon after breaking camp the next morning, we discovered the putrid carcass of an ox steeping in a brook that discharged into the river a short distance above where we had been using the water. During the day we passed the dry beds of a number of ponds or lakes that showed heavy deposits of a whitish crystalized material that was said to be a good quality of common saleratus. We could have shoveled up the stuff by the wagon-load, but, being afraid to use it, did not avail ourselves of the opportunity.

A few miles above Independence Rock is seen another example of Nature's wonder-making, — the Devil's Gate. This chasm is simply a crack across the end of a granite mountain-spur, thirty-five feet wide and three hundred yards long, with walls nearly vertical and four hundred feet high. Through this gorge the Sweetwater forced its way, although the passage was much obstructed by fragments of rock which had broken away and tumbled in from above. On one of the blocks in the middle of the stream lay the remains of a mountain sheep or big-horn. The timid creature, whose favorite haunts are such dizzy heights, had probably become frightened, and thus taken its death-leap from one of the adjacent cliffs. I attempted to pass through the gorge, but my progress was soon arrested. Retracing my steps to an eligible point, I scaled the spur of the mountain, and at the summit observed a dike or cleft about four feet wide cutting the wall down to the river. Rounded, igneous bowlders suggestive of "fire and brimstone" were strewn down the opening, forming an irregular decliv-

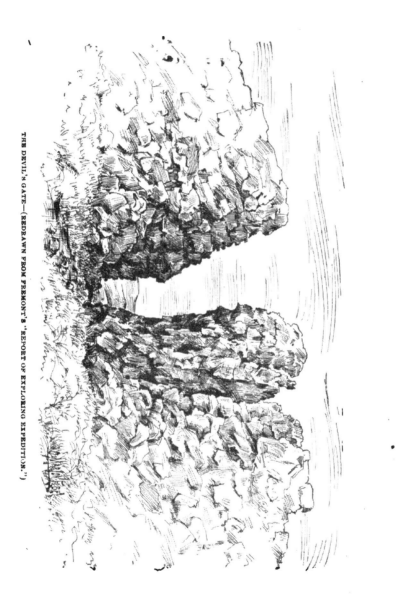

THE DEVIL'S GATE—(REDRAWN FROM FREMONT'S "REPORT OF EXPLORING EXPEDITION.")

ity to the river, as if the *genius loci* had hurled them in
from the top especially for his convenience in travers·
ing the premises. The passage being well travel·
worn, I did not hesitate to undertake the descent.
Well, after clambering for some distance over the
rugged rocks, letting myself down several times from
one projecting bowlder to another, I eventually came
to a point where it seemed impossible to go either for·
ward or backward. But, as it turned out, I escaped
to tell the tale.

Our course now lay along the valley of the Sweetwater for about one hundred miles to the South Pass,
where we crossed the great divide that separates the
waters of the Atlantic and Pacific Oceans. The valley or gateway is from ten to twenty miles wide. The
surface is undulating, occasionally mounting into hills,
and the ascent so gradual that we were scarcely aware
when the culmination was reached and passed. The
bottoms were fairly supplied with grasses; but the uplands were dominated by the now well-nigh ever-pres·
ent sage-brush. As we approached the summit, we
observed several patches of snow near the roadside.
A few varieties of wild flowers were blooming close
by these lingering relics of winter, thus attesting the
aptitude of Nature to respond to her environment what·
ever its character. When upon the summit we were
seven thousand four hundred and ninety feet above
sea-level, and about one thousand miles from our point
of departure on the frontier. To the northward in the
distance the icy crests of the sharp, craggy peaks of
the Wind River Mountains were seen glittering in the

THE WIND RIVER MOUNTAINS.—("REDRAWN FROM FRÉMONT'S "REPORT OF EXPLORING EXPEDITION.")

sun; while far to the southward great snowy ranges lay, like cloud-billows, sleepy and dim upon the horizon.

Just beyond the South Pass we encamped at the Pacific Springs, where for the first time we looked upon water flowing Pacificward. The spring nourished a beautiful, meadow-like park spread out in gentle slopes. The situation was impressive. The great Rocky Range lay between us and home; a vast region to us a terra incognita, stretched away before us. In a less prosaic age, we could readily have peopled the wild, shadowy realm with all sorts of mythical monsters, as was the wont of the old-time Greek when alone musing beside his sea-shore;—

> "At eventide when the shore is dim,
> And bubbling wreaths with the billows swim,
> They rise on the wing of the freshened breeze,
> And flit with the wind o'er the rolling seas."

The trail at this point diverged, one branch going by way of Salt Lake, and the other by way of Bear River. We took the latter branch, which was known as Sublette's Cut-off. Green River, one of the two forks that form the Colorado of the West, was crossed about seventy miles beyond the South Pass. The stream was about four hundred feet wide, with a deep and violent current. Another Mormon had placed a good ferry-boat at this point; so that we had no trouble in getting our wagons over. But the water was so cold and the current so violent that we consumed a whole day in forcing our stock across. Finally, one of the party, Swift from Elkhart, mounting a mule, spurred the animal across, and this broke the way for the herd to follow. The aspect of the river was barren

GRAND HARBOUR

and desolate.   Narrow strips of willow, perhaps a
straggling cottonwood at wide intervals, and occasional patches of grass in the pinched bottoms, made up
about the sum total of its vegetable life.

Between Green River and Bear River we crossed a
divide nearly a thousand feet higher than the South
Pass.   This is the watershed separating the waters of
the Pacific from those of the Great Basin.   We were
now so far above sea-level that the humid atmosphere
afforded sustenance to some of the higher forms of
plant life.   Our road led directly through a small
grove of tamarack, alder, and aspen which crowned one
of the more favored elevations.   This grove was truly
an enchanting spot; at least it so appeared to us after
our thousand miles of timberless monotony.   Comely
trees and shrubs; bright foliage; refreshing shade; fra-
grant flowers; pure, cold springs; sparkling rivulets;
luxuriant grasses; the chirp and chatter of many birds,—
such was the scene as my memory now recalls it.   It
seemed indeed like a precious gem plucked from fairy
land.   No weary, parched and sand-beaten traveler
of Sahara could have been more enraptured upon sight-
ing an oasis than were we upon entering this cheery,
sylvan spot.

The Bear River is the largest tributary of the Great
Salt Lake, and thus belongs to the water system of
the Great Basin.   The section of the route lying along
this stream is one of the few of the journey that I now
recall with pleasurable emotions.   The abundance of
good water, good fuel, and good grazing, were the
characteristics that then most concerned us, though

there was much also in the natural scenery that would have interested the tourist and the scientist. We here saw our first and only geyser. The orifice or throat was about the size of a man's fist, and from this opening at rapid intervals a column of frothing steam and water was ejected into the air a number of feet. After each discharge the water remaining in the orifice could be heard gurgling downward, as if seeking an outlet in the nethermost pit. Near by were the Soda Springs. The water of these readily effervesced with soda, and thus treated made a very palatable drink. Nearly all of these springs, many in number, had built up about themselves cones several feet in height, from the apexes of which, when the flow was not extinct, the water kept up a constant bubbling and spurting. We lay by here over Sunday, refreshing ourselves and teams.

Near where we left the Bear River, at a point where it doubles sharply to the southward in its haste to mingle with the waters of the Great Salt Lake, we were further regaled by seeing a large band of the Sho-sho-ne or Snake Indians. These, too, were an interesting type of the Aborigine. They were migrating nomad-fashion, being generally mounted and carrying with them their families, many ponies, and all their equipments of the camp, the chase, and the war-path. The mounted braves; the fantastic trappings; the squaws with their burdens; the motley households; the pack-ponies; the lodge-poles dragging from the saddles of the ponies; the platform or litter here and there erected on these poles to convey the sick, disabled and infirm; the whooping vaqueros driving the

A BAND OF SHO-SHO-NES MOVING.

loose ponies,—all combined to form a most interesting panorama, and one the like of which is never again to be witnessed in the wilds of this country.

We now at once entered upon a sterile, volcanic plain. According to recent scientific investigations, this plain was a vast lake of molten lava within a comparatively recent geological period. ("Geological Sketches at Home and Abroad," A. Gieke.) I accidentally came upon one of the craters, through which this sea of liquid fire had once been fed from beneath the earth's crust. The aperture was in the form of a long seam or fissure, with irregular walls of black slag-rock, the lips of which were flush with the general face of the plain. I dropped a pebble into the opening, and it went rattling down, bounding from side to side, till the sound, decreasing in volume, was wholly lost in unknown depths.

We were now on the main Oregon emigrant trail; but instead of following this northward to Fort Hall, on Snake River, we soon after leaving Bear River struck to the westward on what was known as Headpath's Cut-off. This route had not been opened till that season, and there were no guide-books to indicate the camping places, as there were for the other roads. We usually carried a keg of water, as a precaution against any dearth of the natural supply, either expected or unexpected; but for several days the region through which we were passing was quite mountainous, and afforded water in such abundance that we began to think it needless to exercise our usual practice of laying in a supply. It so happened that on the very

morning we had neglected to fill our cask, we came
upon a desert stretch of forty miles. Being off duty
I sauntered ahead of the teams. I had also that
morning neglected to fill my canteen, which I usually
carried when not with the teams. It was an arid,
sage-brush plain, which was not only destitute of water, but which had drank every suggestion of moisture
from the atmosphere, and seemed intent on wringing
every object that came within its embrace as dry and
parched as it was itself. It was by far the most trying day's experience I had on the trip. The famish-
ing effects of the situation soon began to tell upon me.
Plodding on and on, stirred with alternating hope and
disappointment upon every apparent change of landscape, I toward the last became so exhausted from
thirst that I was compelled at frequent intervals to
pause for a moment's rest and shelter, even welcoming
for this purpose the presence of the scanty, unsavory,
detested sage-brush.

> "Traverse the desert, and ye can tell
> What treasures exist in the cold deep well;
> Sink in despair on the red, parched earth,
> And then ye can reckon what water is worth."

But the coveted liquid in ample quantity was at length
reached. My companions with the teams came on in
due time, but not of course without both having suffered greatly. It is astonishing how long one, if driven
to the test, will bear up when he would ordinarily think
the last reserve force exhausted.

On this part of the journey, my curiosity led me to
climb a high, commanding eminence, at the foot of
which the road passed, and my toil was happily and

unexpectedly repaid with a fine view of the Great
Salt Lake in the blue distance. Here and there streaks
of dust on the intervening desert plain indicated the
presence of plodding emigrant trains on another route;
as a streak of smoke on the great lakes or on the ocean
indicates the presence of a steamer, though nothing else
than that streak may be
be seen. Those trains
were probably forty to
fifty miles distant. Only
the steady clouds of dust
with their stifling sug-
gestions betokened the
presence of the animate
objects whose tread thus
relieved the sterile though
somewhat picturesque prospect. No
other member of the party was fortunate enough to catch a glimpse of this
only great briny inland sea of our hem-
isphere.

An incident of not quite so poetic a
nature may be related of our experi-
ences on this cut-off. As I have already intimated,
the creature comforts of the plains were not particularly fruitful of the frame of mind that would incline "the brethren to dwell together in unity." So
far as our larder was concerned, we had been for several weeks reduced to bread, bacon, and black, sugar-
less coffee; and the tendency to scurvy had in some
instances begun to disclose itself. We were going

A COOL RECEPTION.

through a narrow canyon, where the road crossed and re-crossed a cold, rapid brook—a branch of Raft River—many times, in picking its tortuous, dubious way. Neal claimed to be ill, and was lying in one of the wagons on an improvised couch with a substratum of a half ton or so of bacon. Rockhill was driving, and, prompted perhaps by waggishness or malice aforethought, capsized the wagon into the icy stream, sousing the invalid into the shivering bath, anchored to the bottom under bacon and all. As might be surmised, that practical joke served effectually to divest that vehicle of its use as an ambulance thereafter.

Nor was this serio-comic scene allowed to go by without its farce, which, if less chilling to the actors, was no less amusing to the bystanders. We encamped shortly after the mishap just mentioned, to dry our drenched goods. One of the men was in the wagon handing down the various articles to another to spread them out on the ground. A quarrel sprang up between the two concerning the ownership of a pillow. They were the same men that had the bout over the apple-sauce back on the Mississippi. The man below happened to be holding a frying-pan in his hand at a moment when his language and manner indicated that he was about to let fly this culinary implement on a mission of vengeance. The other, observing the imminent attitude, seized the water-cask and hurled it at his adversary, shouting with dire vehemence, "D—n you! don't throw that at me!" Happily, the affair terminated, as so many on the route of a similar nature terminated, without physical injury to anyone.

"D—N YOU! DON'T THROW THAT AT ME!"

III.

THE GREAT BASIN.

WE were now, in the heart of the arid wastes of the Great Basin; a region seven to eight hundred miles in width by twice that distance in length and its waters having no visible outlet to the ocean. In general feature this strange country is a high, irregular plateau,[1] liberally studded with bleak and barren mountain peaks and fragmentary ranges, which, in a few instances, approach the dignity and magnitude of systems. Not indeed from the time we entered the Black Hills till we looked upon the blue expanse of the Pacific, did the eye anywhere or for an instant rest upon a spot not hemmed in by mountain barriers. From the Bear River to the Sierra Nevadas, the prospect, as I now look back upon it, was dreary, monotonous, and irksome in the extreme. It struck me as if the Creator, disgusted with His efforts here at world-making, had abandoned His job half finished. Through this region, for about three hundred miles, as we then reckoned the distance, our route lay along the Humboldt River, whose banks from source to mouth were unrelieved by a single tree or even a shrub larger than a stunted willow or sage-brush; and which, finally, as if wearied of its own being, buried it-

---

1 Embraced in past ages a sea, several hundred thousand square miles in extent, say the geologists.

MOONLIGHT CAMP SCENE ON THE HUMBOLDT.

self in the thirsty desert. Horace Greeley, ten years later, in a flying trip through this region by stage, saw
enough of its character to stamp it as the acme of abom-
inations.[1] The emigrants, seeing and knowing more of
it, certainly regarded it with fully as hearty a detesta-
tion, and generally execrated it as the source of their
worst afflictions on the route. But its presence was
very opportune, nevertheless. The journey would
have been much more difficult, if not impossible, without its nourishing help, little as that was. The emigrant sought the river at the earliest practicable moment, and was loth to quit it where its feeble waters
yield up to the desert. The first transcontinental rail-
way was laid out and built along this water course, as
the most feasible route to be found for the purpose.
Indeed, much of this region, despite its barren and desolate aspect, and contrary to the universal opinion held
at that day as to its being utterly worthless, has since
been found to afford fair range for stock, and is now
all utilized by the "cattle barons."

The dwindling down of our party on the plains, one
by one, from six members to three, has already been
mentioned. The circumstances may be noticed here

1 Greeley, in his "Overland Journey," in speaking of the Humboldt River,
among other deprecative things. says: "I only wish to record my opinion that
the Humboldt all things considered, is the meanest river on earth of its length.
. . . Though three hundred and fifty miles long it is never more than a decent
mill-stream. I presume it is the only river of equal length that never had even
a canoe launched upon its bosom. Its narrow bottom, or intervale, produces
grass; but so coarse in structure, and so alkaline by impregnation, that no sen-
sible man would let his stock eat it, if there were any alternative. . . . Half
a dozen specimens of a large, worthless shrub, known as buffalo-bush or bull-
berry, with a prevalent fringe of willows about the proper size for a school-
ma'am's use, comprise the entire timber of this delectable stream, whose gad-
flies, musquitoes, gnats, etc., are so countless and so blood thirsty as to allow
cattle so unhappy as to be stationed on, or driven along this river, no chance

with more particularity. Donahue left us on the Sweet-water, where he joined another party. At the Raft River camp, Good, having become restive at our slow progress, joined James Doane, a home acquaintance, who opportunely overtook us at this point, having come the most of the distance from the frontier on foot; and the two made the balance of the journey in  that manner, packing their mea-gre outfit on their backs. Much better headway was possible traveling in this manner than in any other then available, while little additional discomfort or in-convenience was suffered; since the emigrants that year were supplied with abundance of provisions, and were so thickly strung along the route, probably at that stage of the season all the way from the Missouri River to the Sacramento, that accommodations could generally be obtained when needed. Several weeks later, shortly after we entered the Humboldt Valley, Earl's share of the outfit, including a wagon and two yoke of oxen, was at his request set off to him, when, converting the wagon into a cart, he also parted company with us—finally, as it turned out; so that now of our original party only Rockhill, Neal, and myself remained. We

---

to eat or sleep. . . . Here famine sits enthroned, and waves his sceptre over a dominion expressly made for him. . . The sage-bush and grease-wood, which cover the high, parched plain on either side of the river's bottom, seems thinly set, with broad spaces of naked, shining, glaring, blinding clay be-tween them; the hills beyond, which bound the prospect, seem even more naked. Not a tree, and hardly a shrub, anywhere relieves their sterility; not a brook, save one small one, runs down between them to swell the scanty waters of the river."

kept together till after we reached our destination, when, as will appear hereafter, we too were separated through the exigencies of fortune.

We had now plodded our way to a wearying length. To hitch up and start on with every returning sun had long comprised the chief round of our existence. We came to wonder how we should feel when this trudg- ing routine should be a thing of the past. Thus drag- ging our slow lengths along, fatigued, half-hearted, nauseated with the ever-present sage odor, seeing not a single tree, and having a dreary, inhospitable soli- tude everywhere staring us in the face, we were often prone to ask ourselves whether this sort of life was ever to have an end. One day, when groping along in this passive, pensive, half-forlorn mood, we perchance, on turning a jutting mountain spur, were suddenly awakened, amazed, electrified. We had run upon a party direct from the promised land—straight from the enchanting gold fields. The party proved to be Mormons with their families en route for Brighamland. Their clothing eclipsed any we had ever seen for tat- ters and patches; but their oxen, in striking contrast with ours, were rolling fat and sleek, and thus excited our envy. The members of the party were quite com- municative, and gave us a flaming account of the dig- gings, backing np their words with a liberal display of the shining nuggets. This was the first real, tangible proof we had had of the existence of gold in California. We before believed; we now knew. The effect was ravishing—sent the mercury of our spirits bounding up to the extreme limit of our mental barometers. An

"GLORY HALLELUJAH!   I'LL BE A RICH MAN YET."

elderly member of our party, upon viewing the yellow
metal, could not restrain his enthusiasm; but, capering
about like an exuberant school boy, and shying his hat
into the air, shouted: "Glory Hallelujah! I'll be a rich
man yet." In marked contrast with this little episode,
the words of the plaintive ditty of the gold-miner,
which later actual experience had suggested, came to
my mind times many and oft:

"They told us of the heaps of dust,
And the lumps so mighty big;
But they never said a single word
How hard it was to dig."

Along the Humboldt River, we were annoyed more
or less with the visits of squads of the Digger Indians;
a type chiefly distinguished for their filthy habits, re-
pulsive appearance, and pilfering propensities. Their
inflictions upon the emigrants up to this time had been
chiefly in the way of persistent begging and petty
stealing; but, later in the season, their depredations
took a more serious turn, in the way of running off
and slaughtering stock, and sometimes in attacking
and killing the emigrants themselves. When left to
their own resources, they seemed to subsist mainly on
the fat black crickets of the valley and the plenitude
of their own vermin. On a recent trip by rail through
this section, I saw many of this same species of the redskin gathered about several of the railroad stations.
As at present fed, clothed, and pampered at the expense of Uncle Sam, they show little of the native Dig
ger distinguishing traits.

At the Meadows, on Humboldt River, we took the
Lassen (or Greenhorn) Cut-off. This route struck
northward from this point across the desert, scaled the

Sierra divide near the boundary line between California and Oregon, and then, doubling a sharp angle to
the southward, finally entered the Sacramento Valley
at a point near the present village of Vina, at which
place the present immense Leland Stanford vineyard

is located. We
thus unwittingly
added five hundred
to seven hundred
miles to our jour-
ney, increasing to
that extent the tax
upon our teams, to
say nothing of the
loss of several
weeks of precious
time. Our party,
and that of our whi-
lom captain, John-
son Horrell, had
chanced to fall in
with each other
again. Horrell had
two ox teams. A
party from Missou-
ri with a like outfit
also joined us at

"I COME FROM OLD MISSOURI,
ALL THE WAY FROM PIKE!"—1

1 These lines are from an old-time California comic ballad, which, as sung
from the stage, took California audiences by storm; and thus illustrated in some
degree the levity and ridicule indulged in on the plains and in California in the
early days at the expense of the emigrants from Missouri, seemingly because of
their odd speech, manners, and dress. They were dubbed indifferently as
"Pukes," "Pikes," or "Pike Countians."

about the same time; so that now our train, including our two teams, numbered six wagons, and thus
constituted, we made the balance of the distance to
the Sacramento Valley.

From the Meadows
to Mud Lake, about
a hundred and sixty
miles, the country
was to all appearance
destitute of feed; and
from the Rabbit-Hole
Wells (thirty-seven
miles out) to Mud
Lake, there was no
water except such as
from its temperature
or its mineral proper-
ties rendered it a very
poor makeshift. From
the wells mentioned
to Black Rock, a dis-
tance of forty miles,
there was no water of
any sort. At Black
Rock there was a

JUST FROM "POSEY"—SCENTS GAME.—1

large hot sulphur spring so strongly impregnated that
the atmosphere about the vicinity was surcharged al-

1 The Indianian was known by the pseudonym "Pike Countian," and was
held in little less disfavor than the Missourian, as referred to in the note on
preceding page. The mention of the name "Indiana" or "Hoosier" usually
provoked some half-humorous, half-contemptuous remark about flat-boating
on the Wabash, or about the alleged ill-behavior of the Indiana regiment at the
battle of Buena Vista, the Mexican War being at that time recent history.

most to suffocation with the vaporous brimstone. "Schure, hell ist nicht more es one mile von dis blace," is the by no means inapt ejaculation ascribed to a matter-of-fact son of Teutonia, as he approached this steaming cauldron and sniffed its suggestive odors. The locality was rendered none the more enticing to myself from the fact that, for miles back along the road I had come, I could have stepped almost continuously from the carcass of one dead horse or ox to

COYOTE.

another; so great had been the number of animals that had here perished from hunger, thirst and general exhaustion.[1]

> "For lengthening miles on miles they lie,
> These sad memorials grim and hoary,
> And every whitening heap we spy,
> Doth tell some way-worn pilgrim's story."

Innumerable coyotes, too, attracted hither, snapping, barking, howling, were rendering the situation none the less hideous with their savage orgies over the loathsome carrion.

We made no stop on this forty-mile stretch. Happening to be off duty that day, I wandered alone con-

---

1 I noticed on this stretch the familiar forms of Earl's four oxen, where side by side the pitiable creatures had perished on the desert.

siderably in advance of the teams, and far in the night reached the Black Rock. Groping about the brimstone pool at the foot of this huge, forbidding mass of black lava, in the grim, weird-like starlight, I was startled by stumbling upon an object—it was a man! He was lying among the sage-bushes, wrapped in his buffalo robes. Rousing him up, I learned he was from Elkhart, our neighboring burg, one John Arnold by name. He had been packing through with a party, and, taking ill, was unable to travel farther; so that he was thus left by his companions, sick, penniless, and alone. I remained with him till our teams arrived, when Captain Horrell, being better prepared for the purpose than any of the rest of the party, consented to carry him through, not neglecting however to couple with his motives of benevolence the conditions of what he deemed a good bargain. Most of the emigrants that year were furnished the means to make the journey on condition that they return as compensation a certain share of their earnings during a stated period of time, this share usually being one-half, and the time two years. Horrell exacted for the comparatively small fraction of the journey remaining the same terms that ordinarily were fixed upon at the start. I never heard of Arnold after our dispersion upon reaching the mines till two or three years ago, when I learned that he was living in VanBuren County, Michigan.

We had become accustomed to springs of almost every conceivable variety; but a few miles beyond Black Rock, at our first stop after leaving the Rabbit-

"I WAS STARTLED BY STUMBLING UPON AN OBJECT—IT WAS A MAN!"

Hole Wells, we encamped at the largest and strongest boiling spring of the journey. It threw out a stream several yards in width and of ten to twelve miles in length to the point where it succumbed to the thirsty soil. The water was gurgling, bubbling hot, but when cooled was suitable for use. We had no other for camping purposes, and so availed ourselves of the chilly night air of that region to prepare as large a supply as was possible with our stock of vessels. Rockhill test-ed the temperature several hundred feet below the spring. The water was clear, and went rippling over a pebbly bottom, as harmless to appearance as water

 could be. Rockhill was of an original turn of mind and given to exper-imenting; as Neal was quite free to affirm after his dousing at Raft River.

In yoking up his team he was always utterly indiffer-ent as to how the oxen were mated, or as to the side on which they worked. He had tried the cold water on Neal, and now he would try the hot on the oxen. He made the trial by driving his team through the creek, where he had tested its caloric qualities, and af-fected much surprise when he saw the innocent, unsus-pecting animals fling their hoofs high in the air instant-ly upon touching the water.

Forty miles more of desert brought us to Mud Lake, where, finding abundance of water and grass, we lay by several days to recruit our famished stock. This so-called "lake" we found to be simply an extensive

group of springs whose waters here came to the surface and radiated in rivulets in such manner as to form
a sort of morass containing several hundred acres.
Some of these springs were cold, some hot, and others
represented all the degrees of temperature between
these extremes. I have a very pleasant recollection of
one of the brooks that here took its rise soon to lose
itself in the surrounding desert. This brook was perhaps three feet wide and three feet deep. The bottom
was sandy, the water clear, and just warm enough for
bathing purposes; as I can personally attest from having here enjoyed the most grateful and refreshing bath
of my life. But, as usual, there was not a tree to be
seen; only the everlasting sage-brush.

Twelve miles from Mud Lake, we entered the High
Rock Canyon, which possesses some features that are
unique and striking. It cuts through a range of lava
that is some twenty miles in width and as bare of vegetation as if it had cooled but the day before. The
fissure or gorge that afforded us passage is about the
width of a common road, and is inclosed by high walls
that are carved in irregular outline, as if by the action
of an ancient ice-river. The floor is even, free from
bowlders, and the slope so regular and gentle that it
seems to descend either way from where you stand.
There are few lateral cuts by which egress or ingress
is possible. A fair growth of grass and an occasional clump of the choke-cherry were the sole evidences of life visible. But what appeared the most
remarkable was the acoustic effects, as we verified
by repeated tests. The report of a rifle would go

crashing along the gorge, echoing and re-echoing as if all the genii of the cliffs had been startled and were shouting the alarm one to another and answering it back, till the receding sound died away in the solitude.

This singular lava formation passed, we entered a valley, eight to ten miles in width; the surface of which was ashy-like in color, bore the appearance of a dry lake bed, and was destitute of water and well-nigh of vegetation.[1] On the farther side of this plain, lying directly across our front, and stretching away to the right and to the left as far as the eye could reach, arose a magnificent range of mountains. Looming up abruptly from the plain, and thus being unobscured by the usual foot-hill flankings, this grand upheaval afforded us the most interesting and impressive Alpine view we had yet had on the journey. Our course now lay northward along the base of this range for a number of days before we reached the pass or crossing. Meantime, the same valley formation continued, favoring us with an excellent road-bed, while the side of the adjacent mountain supplied us, in convenient proximity, with luxurious camping places—an abundance of water, timber, and wild clover and other nutritious grasses. We took this lofty divide to be a part of the Sierra Nevada Range, beyond which lay California, the land of our dreams. We became impatient, now that we supposed ourselves so near, that the enchanting

---

1 Rockhill, whose long residence in Nevada, and whose bent for exploration has made him familiar with every part of the Far West, writes me that the alkaline lands of this region, including those of this valley, on which scarce anything else grows, produces an herb known as white sage, which is better for cattle than alfalfa after the frosts come, when they can lick snow as a substitute for water,

prospect should be so long withheld from our vision. Thus impressed, the junior Horrell and myself determined, one day when we were off duty, to scale the barrier and satisfy our craving curiosity. The outcome proved to be another "tenderfoot" exploitation. After climbing laboriously for hours, we finally surmounted what we had taken to be the summit; but, lo, another and still more formidable ascent loomed up grimly and tauntingly before us. Wearied and disgusted, we turned about for the train, determined to abide the regular sequence of events thereafter. When at length we reached the Lassen Pass, we found the altitude still but little diminished, and the gradient very heavy and laborious. We occupied a part of two days in making the passage. A depression at the head of a ravine in the face of the acclivity furnished us a very opportune half-way station for camp and for rest.

ARKANSAW·TOOTHPICK·

IV.

A WELCOME CHANGE.

THIS formidable mountain barrier[1] crossed, we did indeed find a welcome change. The moisture-laden, life-giving breezes from the Pacific, intercepted by this lofty land elevation, had wrought the transformation. The vast desert area, with its wide-spread, death-dealing desolation, was no longer present. Grass, water, and fuel were now abundant. The streams once more went rippling "unvexed" to the sea. The flora at times took on larger forms than we had ever before seen. We passed through miles upon miles of pine forests, whose giant growths were a source of constant surprise and admiration. Still, we were not yet, by any means, to regale ourselves in an ever-recurring Utopia. We yet

---

1 Now known as the Warner Range, and, contrary to what we supposed, and what seems still to be the popular notion, belongs to the Great Basin system, instead of either the Sierras or the Cascades. "The Cascade Range [Capt. C. E. Dutton, *U. S. Geol. Survey*, 1885–86] is usually represented as a northward continuation of the Sierra Nevada. [Fremont so represents it. *Memoirs*, 363.—Author.] In reality an interval of quite a hundred miles separates what may fairly be considered the southern end of the Cascades and the northern end of the Sierra; and, furthermore, if the trend of the Sierra were continuous north-westward, it would pass thirty or forty miles west of the Cascades. The southern end of the latter range may be located with some approach to precision as due east of the base of Shasta." Had Lassen known of this gap, and gone south of the Warner Range, instead of north of it, he would have found, as has since been found, a much shorter and better route than his so-called cut-off.

lacked much of our journey's end; yet had trying experiences before us.

In one particular, at least, our introduction to this side of the range was not at all reassuring. Our first camp was made a few miles below the foot of Goose Lake, from which Pitt River, the principal tributary of the Sacramento, takes its rise. Here, early in the evening, as appeared by the indications, the Diggers raided our stock, taking six of our best oxen; one from each of our six teams, as it happened. The theft was discovered early the next morning, and a detail from our camp at once pushed out upon the

ALLEN "PEPPERBOX."—1 trail of the thieves. The course taken by them was found to lay over a region covered with scrubby cedars and showing a surface so compact that the trail could be distinguished only by the marks made by the oxen's hoofs in displacing the sharp, flinty rock fragments.[2] After the marauders had been thus tracked about twenty miles, the attention of our party was suddenly aroused by a loud shriek from behind a ledge of rocks, and, at about the same instant, a number of redskins were seen, down in a ravine walled in by volcanic bowlders, betaking themselves to their heels as fast as their legs could carry them. But the cowardly flight of the

1 The revolver most seen in '49.--(By courtesy of H. C. Cassidy, Chicago, Ill.)

2 This region has since become known as the Lava Beds, where, in the winter of 1872–78, Captain Jack and his Modocs treacherously slew General Canby and gave the Government such a deal of trouble.

savages was of little avail to us, as every ox had already been put to the knife. Nor was it practicable under the circumstances even to destroy the carcasses; so that, after our departure, the guilty miscreants had only to return at their leisure to enjoy the fruits of their spoil. Our party were indeed fortunate in being able to get out of the affair even as well as they did; for the day was damp and drizzling, and, as was ascertained afterward, not a single gun would have been serviceable, in consequence of the exposure to dampness.

We were now on the California–Oregon wagon road, and, in the course of a few days, met another party from the diggings. This was made up of returning Oregonians, led by General Palmer, a former "Hoosier." Again we were favored with a rose-colored picture of "the chunks so mighty big." A member of the party—a physician—inquired whether we had any saleratus to spare, basing his inquiry upon the assumption that we had laid in a goodly supply from the deposits back on the Sweetwater. When he found we were unable to accommodate him, he was kind enough to inform us that the article was of good quality, and was worth sixteen dollars a pound in the mines; information that came a little late to be of much value to us.

COLT'S PATENT, EARLY PATTERN.—1

---

1 The best side-firearm in '49.—(Lent by J. W. Camper, South Bend, Ind.)

Somewhere in this section a squad of Diggers[1] came to our train, and, seemingly for the first time, laid eyes upon a black man. Their astonishment and curiosity were unbounded. They peered up his sleeves, down his back, into his bosom, and lifted his trousers'-leg, to assure themselves that there was no hoax about the matter—that the cuticle was really black, and black all over. When satisfied as to this, their curiosity turned to contempt and derision—to finger-pointing, jeers, and laughter, evidently greatly to the disrelish of their victim. This same negro, as I learned several years later, turned out to be a much "luckier" money-getter than his ex-owner; and not only purchased his freedom, but also furnished the means to take both his ex-master and himself back to the old Missouri home.

Mention has already been made of the Feather River Meadows, or the Big Meadows, as now known. It was here, it will be remembered, that game was found so plenty, and that Neal brought in seven blacktail deer, and I none. The camp was a truly desirable one in every respect,—grass luxuriant and abundant; timber plenty and convenient; a copious stream of cold, clear, pure water; majestic mountains roundabout; and, withal, a veritable hunter's paradise. We availed ourselves of these rare advantages for several days,

1 The male Diggers of California, at that day, usually went entirely nude. only as they might have happened to don a hat. a shirt, or some other castaway garment of the whites that they had picked up. The squaws wore from the waist to a little below the knees a sort of skirt made of tanned skins. doubled the longer way, and all except the width of about two inches for a waist-belt, cut into "shoe-strings," with shells and other ornaments dangling at the nether ends. The strings of this skirt, or cincture, were sometimes elaborately plaited or woven. and decorated with beads, colored grasses, and various kinds of plumage. The women generally wore what Prof. O. T. Mason described as "the daintiest cap in the world, a hemispherical bowl of basketry made of tough fibre twined with the greatest nicety and embroidered in black, brown, and yellow."

but mainly with the view to prepare for the exigencies that we were forewarned were immediately to follow. For from this point to the Sacramento Valley, some seventy-five miles, the country was, practically speaking, destitute of both feed and water. Over much of this distance, the track crept along on the crest of a very narrow, tortuous divide, or hogback, between two streams buried down in dark, precipitous canyons, more than two thousand feet deep. At one point, the crest became so obstructed with craggy, beetling ledges that it could not be followed at all; thus necessitating the deflection of the trail through a deep hollow, at the bottom of which we were compelled to encamp for the night, without feed or water for our stock, and with only the sage-brush of days agone for fuel.[1]

A DIGGER BELLE.—(FROM A PHOTOGRAPH.)

Rockhill, in spite of the darkness, and by dint of heroic effort, succeeded in picking his way to the creek[2] at the bottom of the can-

---

1 Here, where it was bad enough in all conscience to have to remain a single night, a month or so later, a party of emigrants, including several families, were snowed in and compelled to remain during the entire winter. Among these, were the Reverend William Roberts and family, whose unhappy experiences while thus imprisoned I heard detailed from their own lips.

2 Deposits of rich auriferous gravel were afterward discovered on this stream,—Deer Creek.

yon, and bringing back enough water for our stinted personal needs.

It fell to Neal to take a day at the whip on this exceptional stretch of road. Now, courage and composure under difficulties had little part in Neal's composition. He was always quick to yield the whip to some one else when a bad or dangerous piece of road occurred. But in this instance he had no alternative. I had been taking his relief, as well as my own, for several days consecutively, and, on that morning, stoutly demurred to doing so longer. The sequel was not at all beatifying—to Neal. What with the sharp ridge, the quick curves, the sudden jogs, the obtruding rocks, and the dizzy precipices, he was kept in a constant ferment of fright and excitement. Whipping from one side of the team to the other, and punching the wheel-oxen this way or that, as some dreaded object appeared, constituted his chief diversion for the day. I was trudging along, mute and stolid, behind the wagon, while the most of this grotesque shuttle-cock performance was going on. Neal demanded that I do the punching on one side while he did it on the other; but I was obdurate, protesting that I had asked him for no help when I was in similar straits, and that now he need ask no help from me. The result was, that I was the recipient of much fervid attention at his hands, as he rushed back and forth past me on his frantic rounds. Meanwhile, Rockhill came bowling along in our immediate rear with our other team, with his oxen mated hit or miss as usual, and exhibiting the utmost unconcern as to whether his team or himself was right side up or wrong side up; yet he managed to steer clear of all mishaps, just the same.

We laid in as much hay and water at the Meadows as we were able to carry. Others, of course, took the same precaution. But the supply necessarily fell much short of being adequate, and the strain upon the stock was so great that much of it perished. A train from Columbus, Ohio, were compelled on this account to abandon all their wagons, fifteen in number, and of course the most of their goods, when within less than twenty miles of the Sacramento Valley. Our teams, however, bore up heroically until the worst was over and we were coursing along smoothly upon the bosom of the great valley. But the last straw, so to speak, broke the camel's back. We still had eight to ten miles to water and a camping place. Several of the oxen became exhausted, and one after another sank down in the yoke. We had no recourse but to aban-don them where they lay, and reconstruct our teams as best we could. Thus we worried our way to camp. We were delighted, the next morning, to find the oxen we had left behind grazing upon the wild oats with the rest of the cattle, as if nothing had happened. The coolness of the night had so refreshed them that they became able to follow us to feed and to water. Many of the outfits improvised from the salvage of the wrecks on the plains, similar to our own, but worse, would have been quite amusing, had they not told so serious a story. It was no uncommon thing to see emigrants—perhaps families—come in off the plains having all their worldly effects that they had been able

to save packed in an abbreviated cart drawn by a cay-
use harnessed with a cow or an ox, or even upon the
back of a single ox or cow.

"D—N THE HUMBOLDT!"

This camp was at Lassen's ranch, where Peter Lassen had erected a log cabin, and was keeping a small
stock of staple goods. This was the first sign of civilization we had seen for many a day. It was a motley
scene of emigrants, Indians, old-time Californians, etc.,
that greeted our vision. Not many rods away flowed
the poetic river—the Sacramento,—of whose "glittering sands" we had sung upon leaving home. We were
not long in hastening down to gaze upon its crystal,
magic waters. It was a moment of strange, deep,
soul-stirring emotions as we first stepped upon its
banks. Was this indeed our journey's end?—this the
goal of our many weary days, weeks, and months of
toil, privation, peril? Had we undergone some Pytha-
gorian transformation of soul, we could scarce have
felt more strange, fanciful, etherial. The eleventh day
of October! Yes, seven months and nineteen days
since we began the journey. It had been a truly event-
ful period in life's brief span; an episode of quaint, va-

ried, and impressive scenes, incidents, and experiences, which must ever remain stamped in vivid outline on memory's tablet.

We had been singing, as already mentioned, of the "glittering sands" of the Sacramento. We were now, of course, anxious to verify our long-cherished anticipations. There, surely enough, were "glittering sands" dazzling upon the eye, as the current whirled the flaky particles over and over in the sunlight. Were these particles gold?—were these really the "sands" we were to gather with wash-bowls on our knees? We would fain believe, but could not trust our senses. Captain Horrell had been to us a sort of Sir Oracle in all things. The Captain, moreover, had been a diligent student in geology and mineralogy all the way out. We envied him his knowledge in these now practical sciences. He would have, we were sure, much the advantage of us in discovering and identifying the precious stuff. The Captain was, therefore, at once besought to enlighten us as to the composition of these drifting atoms. The moment his ready eye was focused upon the sparkling objects, he exclaimed, with an air of perfect assurance: "Oh, yes; those are gold; but the particles are too fine to pay to gather them." It turned out that the bright flakes were simply scales of mica, mingled with the other ingredients of disintegrated granite, of which substances the lower bottoms of the river are almost wholly composed.

We were still fifty to sixty miles from the point where we decided to locate,—Redding's Diggings. A conspicuous landmark on this short journey was the great white dome of Shasta Butte. Rising directly in our front, and far overtopping all the other peaks and ranges within our scope of vision, it constantly challenged attention, though we were at no time less than seventy to eighty miles away.

"Behold the dread Mount Shasta, where it stands
Imperial midst the lesser heights; and, like
Some mighty impassioned mind, companionless
And cold."

This huge pile is said to be visible from Monte Diablo—two hundred and fifty miles, "as the crow flies;"

SHASTA BUTTE.—(FROM A PHOTOGRAPH.)

and, today, "from the dome of the capitol at Sacramento, it meets the eye of many a gazer who knows not its name or the great distance it lies to the north. The mariner on the ocean can see it, and emigrants on the parched deserts of Nevada have traveled toward it day after day, an infallible guide to lead them on to the land of gold." Little wonder, therefore, that the "Poet of the Sierras," standing on the summit of this monarch of the mountains, in a presence suggestive of the thunderbolt, the volcano, the avalanche, and the earthquake, should thus give wing to his fancy:

"I stood where thunderbolts were wont
To smite thy Titan-fashioned front;
I heard large mountains rock and roll ;
    I saw the lightning's gleaming rod
Reach forth and smite on heaven's scroll
    The awful autograph of God."

We pitched our camp at the extreme head of the Sacramento Valley, upon very nearly, if not exactly, the site of the present town of Redding. These mines were known as "dry diggings," which were worked chiefly with pick, spoon, and pan, there being no water convenient to run the rocker or the long-tom. The diggings, so fer as our experience went, "panned out" decidedly "dry" indeed. During our week's trial, we averaged hardly a dollar a day to the man; and our geological and mineralogical expert did no better than the rest of the party. My first experience was to prospect a "pot-hole," which I discovered in winding my way up the dry bed of a gulch, which had been scooped and swirled out through a hard granite ledge. I imagined that the nuggets, in being swept down the channel during freshets, would surely have lodged in a receptacle so convenient and befitting, and wondered that so promising a "lay-out" had not been discovered before. The pot-hole, or pocket, proved to be shaped like an inverted balloon; and it took a half day's vigorous, feverish labor at my hands to reach the bottom, when with bated breath I discovered—well, not even so much as the "color." Any experienced miner would have known beforehand that such would be the outcome. We all became thoroughly disgusted with our "luck" here; and Rockhill, Neal, and myself determined upon a change of base.

We were informed that at Sacramento—everybody called it Sacramento *City* in those days—sixteen dollars per cord was the current price paid for wood-chopping; and, being all of us accustomed to the woods and the ax, we at once decided to head for that point, which was about a hundred and seventy-five miles distant. Good had rejoined us since our arrival off the plains, and was at the time away prospecting with ex-Governor Redding and party. But we were too impatient of delay to await his return. By arrangement, Neal and I started ahead on foot, and Rockhill was to follow with the team. The Sacramento River was forded a short distance above the mouth of Antelope Creek, both as we went up and as we returned. Near the ford, we were treated to a California *rodeo*, or round-up, with the accompanying process of cattle-branding, which was the first exhibition of that sort we had ever seen. The vaqueros appeared all to be trained Indians. A calf would be singled out from the herd and pursued by several of the vaqueros, each swinging his coiled lariat over his head, and yelling with the vehemence of true savagery. The animal was soon ensnared about the head or the neck from opposite sides by two of the horsemen, when a third horseman came up from the rear and threw a noose around the hind legs. The three lariats, each secured to the pommel of a saddle, were now drawn taut in different directions, which threw the victim, and held it securely while the branding-iron (*heirro*) was pressed into the quivering flesh. It was all the work of but a moment.

At about this point, the rainy season began, and began in earnest. In a few days the most of the streams were out of their banks, and the valley had become next to impassable for teams. Neal and I, however, worried our way forward till we reached Long's Bar, on Feather River. We found a state of things here far from comforting. The river was a roaring torrent, and the ferry-boat had been swept away and drowned the ferry-man the day before our arrival. The camp was made up chiefly of emigrants,

THE OLD-TIME CALIFORNIA VAQUERO.

and was very nearly destitute of provisions. The most of the teams had been sent to Sacramento for winter supplies; but the floods and bottomless roads had made it impossible for them to return. We had expected to meet a home acquaintance at this camp, which had aroused in us vivid conceptions of "square meals" and other bodily comforts. But, when within a mile or two of the place, we met that same acquaintance hobbling up the mountain side. He had a gun on his shoulder;

had just come out of a severe spell of sickness, he said; was out of "grub;" and wanted to see if he couldn't kill a jack-rabbit or something else to relieve his gaunt stomach. A more forlorn picture than he presented could scarcely be imagined. We had now ourselves got down to our last fifty cents. Neal succeeded in getting employment, at four dollars per day and board. I went down to the four-by-six tent, where he was stopping, to bid him good-bye. I found him standing in front of the tent in the rain, warming over a batch of boiled beans in a frying-pan, which was the sum total he had for his breakfast. He, meanwhile, kept up a vigorous whistling, as if to compensate for the meagreness of his meal, and to dispel the melancholy, if not the ludicrousness, of the situation.

We arranged that I should push forward to Sacramento, and that he should follow in four days. I, accordingly, took our cash balance and struck out for the city, afoot and alone. The first night out, I made my camp under a friendly oak, without fire or food. It rained almost continuously during the whole trip. My only protection was a pair of Mackinac blankets. These I threw over my shoulders to protect me from the rain by day, and I rolled up in them to sleep the best I could by night. All the ferry-boats on the river were adrift, so that I was unable to cross for several days. Very opportunely, I came upon a party of three men, who with their team were detained on account of the condition of the roads. They were from Michigan. Their stock of provisions consisted of flour, and flour only. This they made into mush, which they

generously shared with me.   Finally, a man came up
the river in a yawl after some hay.   I assisted him in
his work, and he reciprocated by taking me down the
river and landing me on the opposite side, at Fremont;
an ambitious city in embryo at the junction of the
Feather and the Sacramento Rivers.   The only resources of this "city" seemed to be town lots.   I was
not at all in a speculative mood at the time; and, though
it was late in the day, I struck out at once across the
open plain for Sacramento.   The trip was not under-
taken as if it were by any means to be a pleasure
jaunt.   Night came on, and, after pushing along a
number of hours, a light appeared ahead in the distance.   The sight was a most welcome one; but, on
arriving upon the scene, my joy was quickly dispelled.
Here, in the mid-plain, were a man and his wife, with

their wagon swamped, and
their oxen in the mire, 'dead.
The couple were headed for
the mines with their winter's
stock of provisions, and were
thus hopelessly stranded.   The
road was strewn with many
evidences of similar sad experiences.   I must myself have
cut a ludicrous, if not a pitiable, figure, as I went plashing
along through the rain and
mud and slush, with my blankets over me, my boots across
my shoulder, my pants rolled

up to my knees, my white wool hat gone to seed clown-
fashion, and myriads of ducks, geese, and brants quawk-
ing and flapping their wings over my head. But,—

"Come what come may,
Time and the hour runs through the roughest day."

The American River was at length reached. It took
my last two-bits—a dime and a Spanish shilling—for
ferriage; so that I entered Sacramento in a worse
predicament than Doctor Franklin's when he entered
Philadelphia,—had no pennies for loaves, to say nothing of a whistle.

V.

STRANGE SCENES AND EXPERIENCES.

———

THE appearance of Sacramento was truly unique. Nearly or quite all the buildings were made of canvas tacked upon poles. It was practically at the head of navigation on the Sacramento River, and was thus the entrepot for the central and the northern mines. All was intense bustle and excitement. A very hotly contested election[1] was in progress, which still further intensified the situation. Here, intermingled and jostling each other, were representatives from every quarter of the globe, all moved by the one engrossing purpose,—GOLD.

"Extremes of habits, manners. time, and space,
Brought close together. here stood face to face;
And gave at once a contrast to the view,
That other lands and ages never knew."

It was surprising to note the facility with which men adapted themselves to the new conditions. A physician of my acquaintance I found engaged in draying.

1 Held on November 13, when members of Congress were elected and a complete State government was set up, in pursuance of a constitution framed and adopted by the people, without authorization by Congress, the only instance of the sort in our history. The firm stand taken in this constitution for freedom was, as noticed incidentally by Gen. Bidwell in a letter to the writer, the first decisive event in that series of momentous historic movements that ultimately culminated in the destruction of slavery and the fruition of a united and homogeneous country.

The lawyer, who had so gallantly come to my defense back on the plains, greeted me from the top of a high rick of sacked flour, which he was crying off at auction. A preacher, who had parted with us early on the route, because we sometimes traveled of Sundays when we did not have suitable camping places to lay over, had changed the pulpit for the saloon. There was little leisure for choosing an occupation; the first opportunity offered had to be laid hold of, for a time at least. My first and only job in the city lacked much of being to my fancy. Since leaving my Michigan friends on the Feather River, I had had nothing to eat. My appetite, therefore, had become so keenly whetted that I took my place among the guests at the first table I

FROM A PHOTOGRAPH.   SEE PAGE 90.

saw, taking my chances as to what might follow. This was at Knight's Hotel, probably the best of its kind in the city, though constructed of canvas, like the rest of the makeshifts about it. One of the proprietors stood in the door to attend to the guests as they departed. This rendered the situation a little ominous for me; but, after fully satisfying my inner-

man, I at once approached this dignitary as an appli-
cant for work. He quickly responded, "Yes; have
you had your dinner?" I replied that I had. He
thereupon immediately put a man in his place, and bid
me follow him to the boat-landing, where I shouldered
up several rough boards and packed them to the rear
of the hotel. Here, clad in dirty red flannel shirts and
blue overalls, and lying upon a board outdoors, exposed to the pelting rain, were the re-mains of two
miners. I was set at work mak-ing two box-boards I
had es from the carried up for the bur-ial of these
bodies; and that is the way I paid for my din-ner. The
spectacle, as well as the job, was far from delec-table,
espe-cially as I was at the time afflict-ed with the same
com-plaint of which these

FROM A PHOTOGRAPH.   SEE FOOT-NOTE, PAGE 89.

John Bidwell

poor fellows had died. Dysentery of a malignant type
was prevalent; and, as the doctors had not learned how
to treat the disease as modified by that environment,
the mortality from this cause was very great. Later,
such gruesome spectacles, I was told, were of every-
day occurrence about this establishment; so common
indeed as no longer to invoke coffin, winding-sheet, or
ceremony of any sort, save the dray and spade, as the

SUTTER'S FORT, 1849.

carcass of a dog would be treated. Many of these, no
doubt, were well-to-do at the far-away home, where all
the cherished endearments of family and friends were
awaiting their return; but, it may be, that the record-
ing angel alone will ever know of their hapless end
on earth.

"How little do we know of what we are,
How less, of what we may be!"

Two miles from the Sacramento, and east of the
city, was the famous   Sutter's Fort,[1] which up to
that season had been   the terminus of the only
overland wagon trail   entering California, and
which for nearly a de-

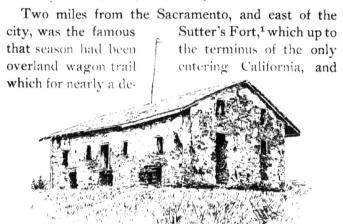

SUTTER'S FORT, 1890.—(FROM A PHOTOGRAPH.)

cade had been the focal point of the American residents
of the country. Hence, probably, the name of the
river near by,—Rio de los Americanos. The fort was

1 General John Bidwell, of Chico, Cal., a pioneer of '41, who was long con-
nected with this fort as Sutter's general manager, and who retains a vivid
recollection of its plan in detail, has kindly furnished me with an outline sketch
and other valuable data to aid in the drawing of this cut, which he upon examining the proof pronounces substantially correct and a much truer picture than
any of the many others that had come to his notice. I revisited the site of this
fort in 1884, and was pained to note that the central two-story adobe building
was all that remained of this monument of a unique and picturesque past. This,
too, was wholly neglected and in an advanced state of decay. A more appre-
ciative public, however, has quite recently restored the whole structure, of
which I have received a photograph since I wrote the foregoing.

established by Captain John A. Sutter (1803–1880) as
the headquarters of his great rancho, upon which he
had other improvements, including the saw-mill, at
which the gold was discovered.   Captain Sutter was
an ex-officer of the Swiss army, emigrated to this
country in 1838, lived in Indiana for a while, and, finally, after several years of adventure, found his way to
California, in 1840.   He is said to have been liberal
and hospitable to a fault.   "Everybody was welcome—
one man or a hundred, it was all the same."   Yet, it
was his grim fate to die upon the verge of pauperism.

The wood-chopping project not turning out as expected, I again set face for the mines, a friend having
loaned me the wherewith for the purpose.   I did not
wait for Neal, and it was well that I did not; for he
drifted elsewhere, and I saw him no more.   Nor did I
again meet Rockhill until I met him at home, seven
years thereafter.   I then, for the first time, learned of
his fate after we separated at Redding's.   He had not
been able, in consequence of the floods, to get the team
any farther than Deer Creek, where he left all the property in charge of a ranchman, one Colonel Anthony
Davis; and, in the Spring, when an accounting was
sought, both ranchman and property had disappeared,
not again to be found.[1]

I now headed for Coloma, about fifty-five miles distant, of course still "tramping" it.   At all stations
along the road, beginning with the Ten Mile House,
meals were two dollars each.   The lodging accommo-

---

1 A statement which I was pleased to have verified thirty-five years later,
through my accidental meeting of the ranchman's widow in another and distant part of the state.

dations were overtaxed at every point. At Shingle Springs, I paid a dollar for the privilege of lodging in a covered cart, in company with a barrel of pork. It was raining hard, and that was the only alternative. Of course one had to furnish his own bedding in those

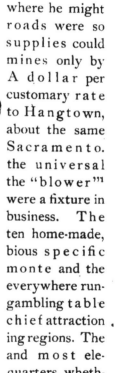

days, no matter where he might lodge. The roads were so wretched that supplies could be got to the mines only by pack-animals. A dollar per pound was the customary rate to Coloma and to Hangtown, which were about the same distance from Sacramento. Gold dust was the universal currency, and the "blower"[1] and the scales were a fixture in every place of business. The weights were of· ten home-made, and of very dubious specific gravity. The monte and the faro tables were everywhere running flush. The gambling table indeed is the chief attraction in all new mining regions. The most pretentious and most elegantly furnished quarters, wheth-

THE TYPICAL OLD-TIMER.—2

er tents by the roadside or palaces in a city, are dedi-

1 A shallow sort of tray, usually of tin, triangular-shaped, with one corner open, used to blow black sand and other foreign substances from gold dust, and to handle the dust about the scales

2 The "Panama" hat, silk sash, embroidered shirt, and absence of vest and coat—somewhat after the Mexican style—made up a costume much affected in

cated to this purpose. Such resorts are, in fact, about the only places in such regions where men can pass their leisure hours or find companionship and recreation. 'Tis ever thus,—Brazen Vice rears his gilded temples before Modest Virtue scarce thinks of breaking ground. The brood of "suckers" was especially bountiful while the inflow of the annual overland emigration lasted.

"Could fools to keep their own contrive,
On what, on whom, could gamesters thrive?"

FROM A PHOTOGRAPH.

Jas. W. Marshall

THE DISCOVERER OF GOLD AT SUTTER'S MILL.

My first halt was at a double-log house, on the Sacramento-Coloma road, a mile or two west of the latter place. It was called the "Mountaineers' Home," and was a sort of tavern and trading-post combined. My chief occupation while here was cutting house logs at a dollar each and wood at five dollars per cord, the latter from brittle and crooked oaks. Board was six dollars per day, the sumptuous fare consisting of bacon, beans, coffee, and musty-sog-

those days; and was the object of awe and admiration of the "tenderfoot," who looked upon the chaps thus pompously clad as being already surfeited with the precious dust. Everybody had also a penchant for gibbering Spanish. The typical miner, as usually represented in the prints, is mere caricature, the shabby clothes and the unkempt person being no more than the natural result of the neglect and indifference that men drop into in the absence of society everywhere.

gy-buggy-wormy bread. Flour was two dollars per pound, and a villainous article at that, the most of it having made the voyage round Cape Horn and heated in the ship's hold. Potatoes were eight dollars per pound, the chief use to which they were put being as a cure for scurvy, which complaint was then quite common. The locality was in the very heart of the best diggings in California, but we did not know this at the time. We often picked up good-sized nuggets in the door-yard after a heavy rain; but it did not occur to any of us to prospect for diggings, either there or anywhere else in the flat of several acres in which the cabin was

FROM A PHOTOGRAPH.

H. W. Bigler.[1]

situated. My recollections of the place are cherished none the more because of the presence of a victim of delirium tremens, who imagined that he was in hell suffering the torments of the damned, while just beyond him, in plain view, was heaven, with the angels in the full ecstacy of bliss. Another incident of the place

---

1 Henry W. Bigler, St. George, Utah; Azariah Smith, Manti, Utah; and James S. Brown and William Johnson, Salt Lake City, Utah, all Mexican War veterans, and ex-members of the famous Mormon Battalion, which was mustered out in California, in 1848, are the only survivors of the gold discovery party now known to me. Peter L. Wimmer, of San Diego, Cal ; and Wilford Hudson, of Grantsville, Utah, also of that party, were living, according to "The Century," in 1891; but I do not know whether they are living now—1895.

may be worth relating, as indicative of the social state of the time. One evening, as we were sitting about our generous chimney-fire, a guest dropped in upon us for the night. He was a striking character—young, dark complexioned, dashing, of splendid physique, and of pleasing, cultured address. He was partly dazed from the effects of an easy, nonchalant manner, gave us his story, in brief as follows: He had belonged, he said, to a detachment of United States regulars, which was crossing the plains that season to Oregon. When near the junction of the California and Oregon roads, he took French leave, and, appropriating two of the best army hors-

FROM A PHOTOGRAPH.   SEE FOOT-NOTE, PAGE 93.

es, had made his way to the Golden State. Just now, he had emerged from the culminating scene in a series of other adventures. There were many cattle roaming at will on the plains about Sacramento that winter, and wagons and other team appurtenances were easy of access about the city. From these sources he became possessed of a four-ox team, on the same principle that he had become possessed of the two Government horses. Thus equipped, he sought and obtained a load of freight for the mines, for which he was to receive a dollar per pound for transportation. But he diverted from the proper destination, and fetched up at Mormon Island, where he sold both team and goods, and pocketed the proceeds. He next turned up at Coloma. Here he fell in with a German, who was about to leave for *Das Vaterland*, and who was fond of displaying a bulky purse of nuggets, with which he intended to set the crowds abroad agape. The upshot was: the German missed his nuggets, and his new-made friend was accused, tried in a "people's court," convicted, and sentenced to a hundred lashes, half to be given at once, and the rest af-

FROM A PHOTOGRAPH. SEE FOOT-NOTE, PAGE 83.

ter a week's respite. When he came to us, he had just undergone the last installment. From his raw and bleeding back, it was evident that the thong had been robustly applied, and the victim vowed eternal vengeance upon the merciless hand that did it. The fellow, however, with refreshing facetiousness, justified the deed, upon the ground that no such fine American gold should be allowed to be taken from the country!

Coloma, as is well known, is located on the South
Fork of the American River, and is distinguished his-
torically as the place where, on January 24, 1848, James
W. Marshall, in examining the tail-race of the Sutter
sawmill, made the gold discovery, which set the world
ablaze, and was so far-reaching and momentous in its
results. I saw the mill many times. It was of the old-
fashioned, flutter-wheel, sash-saw model,[1] and was
pounding away day and night while I knew it. It was
situated a little below the town on an extensive bar,
which, through many re-workings, has since been almost wholly washed away; and thus, through these en-
croachments of the eager, unsentimental gold-seeker,
the old mill, and the race below it, where the first piece
of gold was picked up, have long since disappeared.
Even the exact site of the mill can no longer be point
ed out.

> "Yet, the years may chase each other
>   Down the rugged steeps of time,
> The world may lose its harmony,
>   Life's song its merry rhyme;
> But forever and forever
>   The story of the mill
> And the man who dug the mill-race,
>   Will linger with us still."

Marshall's discovery at the mill was not, it appears,
the result of mere accident. The water-wheel had
been set too low, and the water was being let into the
tail-race of nights to cut out the channel so as to free
the wheel. It was Marshall's custom to walk along
the race in the morning, after the water had been shut

1 I have been at considerable pains to get an accurate picture of this mill,
having had before me several cuts said to have been sketched on the spot from
the original, among which is the print in "California Illustrated," by G V.
Cooper, and a pencil sketch by C. B. Gillespie. I have also availed myself of
suggestions from Gillespie, H. W. Bigler, St. George, Utah, and Azariah Smith,

SUTTER'S MILL, SCENE OF THE GOLD DISCOVERY.

off, so as to give the men directions in the work. On the
day previous to the discovery, a section of bed-rock
in the race, laid bare by the water, excited his curiosity; and, calling one of his men[1] to him, he, after drawing attention to this queer-looking rock, remarked that
he believed there was gold thereabouts, this belief being founded on the fact, he said, that he had noticed
the "blossom of gold" (quartz) in the adjacent hills,
and that he had read in some book that the presence
of quartz was a sign of gold. So strong was he in
this belief that he sent the man to the cabin for a pan,
that he might make the test, by washing some of the
sand and gravel from the tail-race. The test was un-
successful; but the failure did not satisfy Marshall.
"Well," he said to his attendant, "we will hoist the
gates tonight and let in all the water we can, and to-
morrow morning we will shut it off and come down
here, and I believe we will find gold or some other
mineral." As he was a rather eccentric sort of man,
no heed was paid to this seeming whim. But Marshall
was in a different frame of mind. The next morning
at an unusually early hour some one was heard pounding at the mill. It was Marshall. "There was at the
time a carpenter's work-bench standing in the mill-
yard; a little way from it was a saw-pit for whip-saw-
ing lumber; also men at work in the mill-yard fram-

Manti, Utah, the latter two of whom assisted Marshall in building the mill.
The conspicuous forebay in the Nahl design, as printed in "The Century," appears to be merely an embellishment by the artist; for the water entered the
mill from the front or east side. and not from the right or north side.

1 This man was James S. Brown, whose portrait is printed on page 95, and
the facts narrated down to the quotation "There was at the time a carpenter's
work-bench," etc., I glean from his interesting pamphlet entitled, "California: An
Authentic History of the First Find," published by himself, Salt Lake City, Utah.

ing timbers and hewing with a broadaxe. Near the flutter-wheel there was a large bowlder to be blasted out. I was at the drill preparing to put in a blast of powder when Marshall came up from the tail-race carrying his slouch hat in his arms, and, setting it on the work-bench, exclaimed: 'Boys, I believe I have found a gold mine.' At once the men gathered around, and sure enough in the top of his hat, the crown knocked in a little, was the pure stuff in small pieces or rather thin scales. All knew it was gold, although not one had ever seen the metal before in its natural state."[1] It was agreed on all hands that the discovery should be kept secret; but the news took wing in spite of all precautions to the contrary. The public, however, were slow to believe, so that it was some time before the importance of the event came to be realized.

The holidays found me at Hangtown, which took its suggestive name from the circumstance that two men—a Frenchman and a Spaniard—were hanged here, for robbery and murder. The process was in pursuance of the usual miner's code, and occupied but twenty-four hours for its complete execution. The oak that did duty on the occasion may be seen in the annexed plate, between two buildings, nearly opposite the "El Dorado," from whose tall flag-staff a streamer is flying. In the fall of '50 the camp was the scene of another hanging-bee, the process being much more summary than that just mentioned. The subject was "Irish Dick," who killed a man across a gambling table in the "El Dora-

---

1 This last quotation is from a letter by Henry W. Bigler to the author dated St. George, Utah, May 31, 1894. See portrait and note, p. 93.

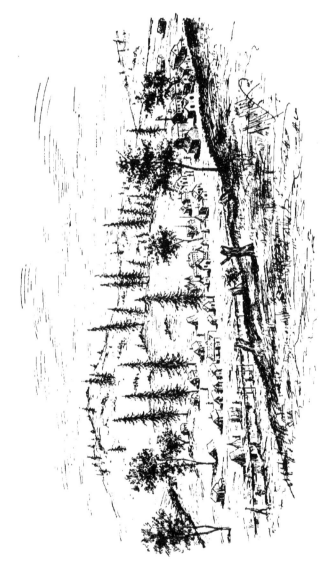

HANGTOWN.—(AFTER A CUT IN, "CALIFORNIA ILLUSTRATED.")

do." The crowd on the inside, in less time than it takes to tell it, seized the wretch and thrust him out the door to the quickly assembled crowd on the outside, when a noose was put about his neck and he was hurried off to the most convenient tree. The other end of the rope was thrown over a limb and grasped by a number of men, when the fellow was asked if he had anything to say. He coolly took a monte deck from his vest pocket, and began to shuffle the cards, saying, "If anybody wants to buck, I'll give him a layout." A quick haul upon the cord, and a graceless, conscienceless villain dangled in the air.[1]

---

1 "Dick" was brought across the plains the previous season by one of my partners, and was a slim strippling of about twenty, thin visaged, and with large, uneven teeth, and a slight Irish accent. He drew a dirk upon me as we were going up street one evening because of some pleasantry of mine; but I had no thought then that he was capable of murder.

VI.

THE PICK AND SHOVEL AGAIN.

————

HANGTOWN was, at this period, one of the most important mining camps in the State. Claims were limited to fifteen feet square; so the miners could not work long in a place. Two men usually formed the ephemeral mining partnerships, as by the methods of mining then in vogue that number could generally work together the most profitably. The best diggings I "struck" about here were on Hangtown Creek, a half mile below town, where my partner and I took out, for awhile, with a long-tom,[1] fifty to a hundred dollars apiece per day. We also found good mines in Kelsey's Canyon, in which the gold was mainly flax-seed shaped, and of a very uniform and beautiful variety. The largest piece I ever found was in a "gutted" gulch, in the grease-wood hills, westward of town. Here, with the first stroke of the pick, I raked out of the clay an ounce chunk, and with the next stroke, one weighing two and a quarter ounces.[2] This was certainly encouraging

1 The first long-tom I saw was in the spring of '50.
2 Gold was usually found in small particles, but it ranged from the size of almost impalpable powder up to very large nuggets. In September, 1871, a piece worth $6,000 was taken out by Bunker & Co., in the State of Oregon,

for a beginning; but there was no water near, and the beginning proved also to be well-nigh the end. But, as a rule, mining, even at that day, could not, by any means, be reckoned a profitable employment. A lady who kept boarders in Hangtown, in the winter of '49–50, informed me that very few of her boarders paid or were able to pay; and one of these boarders, who applied himself very diligently, owned to me that he had not taken out as much as a quarter of an ounce on any day during the winter.[1]

The diggings where the large nuggets were found, and where there were several cabins, were entirely deserted at the time of our operations there; as was also Kelsey's Canyon. The notion generally entertained during the winter of '49–50, was that higher up in the Sierra lay *in situ* the original "big lumps," of which the flakes and other small particles lower down were but the float or waste. Many were the extravagant yet fully credited rumors whispered about from friend to friend as to the pound-a-day diggings that, up there, invitingly awaited the advent of spring to open up their treasures. Accordingly, when that longed-for time came round, the real mining belt was almost wholly deserted, in the stampedes for those fancied ophirs. My partner and I, not to be left napping under such circumstances, were among the very first to break from this camp. We went by the Carson emi-

which is perhaps the largest specimen ever found on the Pacific Coast; but we have an account of much larger finds in the Australia mines, one discovered in the Donolly district, in 1869, weighing 2,520 oz., and worth $48,000.

1 Doubtless many old miners would agree with Brigham Young in the declaration he made to the Colfax party, in 1865, "that every dollar of gold taken out in the United States had cost one hundred dollars."

NEAR THE BACKBONE OF THE SIERRA.—(ADAPTED FROM "PACIFIC TOURIST."

grant trail as far as Leek Springs, at which point we
found ourselves up among the branches of the stately
sugar pines, on the crust of the snow, which was so
solidly packed that our horse's hoofs made just indentation enough to make it comfortable traveling.   At
this point the backbone of the Sierra was in plain view
and apparently but a few miles away.   Swathed in
winter snows of untold depth, as it now was, this great
divide wore a most ominous and forbidding aspect,
and sent a shudder of awe through the soul as we con-
templated its awful majesty:

"With foundations seamed and knit,
    And wrought and bound by golden bars,
Sierra's peaks serenely sit
    And challenge heaven's sentry-stars."

Well, it was on the South Fork of the American River, or on a tributary thereto, somewhere in this region,
that we were to find a party of miners that had been
rolling out the pound chunks the whole winter long.
That is to say, it had confidingly come to our ears
that some one had affirmed that he had seen a man
who had heard another man say that he knew a fellow
who was dead sure that he knew another fellow who,
he was certain, belonged to a party that were thus
shoveling up the big chunks—or something to that effect.   We now, of course, knew that we had been
hoaxed; yet it was, doubtlessly, all round a case of—

"Themselves deceiving and themselves deceived."

But our frank and earnest avowals as to the facts made
not the slightest impression upon the party after party
we met on our return, that, having got wind of our
slipping away, were on our track, determined upon

sharing in our supposed "good thing." They became convinced only when they saw the imprints of our horse's hoofs in the snow where we had turned about from our fool's errand. And, forsooth, such is about as rational a foundation as miners' stampedes have usually had from that day to this. For, be it known, that of all men the gold-miner is proverbially the readiest—

"To swallow gudgeons ere they're catched,
And count the chickens ere they're hatched."[1]

Another notion then widely prevalent was, that, as the river-bars were rich in auriferous deposits, the river-beds should be much more so, especially in the deep-water stretches between the rapids. Hence, in the summer of 1850 a large percentage of the miners clubbed together to turn the various rivers of the mining-belt from their beds, at the more favorable points, by means of canals, or flumes, or both, as necessity required. One such company was organized to drain the South Fork at Spanish Bar, opposite Placerville. The conditions here, as the theory ran, were precisely what was desired. Here was the deep-water stretch, and into this emptied the Hangtown and the Kelsey Canyons, both of which were very rich. On the

1 The Sun River stampede in Montana, in the fall of 1865, may be cited as a typical instance. One McClellan had discovered a very rich gulch on the west side of the Range, and had thus acquired considerable fame locally as a prospector. He was afterward, at the time above-mentioned, leaving Helena with two mules packed with provisions A friend accosted him as to his destination. "Oh;" he replied *soto voce* and with a sly twinkle of the eye. "I've got as good a thing out here as I want, this winter," The news of this incident got abroad, and touched off the percussion gold-hunters within reach, occasioning the most notable stampede of the country. When the rush was well under way, a tremendous blizzard came up, causing much and intense suffering. Four men were brought back frozen stark dead, and many had limbs or other members more or less seriously frozen. Now, it turned out that all McClellan had meant by his pleasantry was that somewhere out in the Sun River wilds, he had put up a cabin for the winter and taken to himself an Indian wife.

strength of this favorable prospect, a large force of men spent the season in turning the river and pumping out the hole, when, to their great surprise and disappointment, but a few hundred dollars were realized, and this was at the mouth of the Hangtown Canyon, where evidently it had been but recently deposited. Such, generally, was the outcome of similar ventures that season; so generally, indeed, that the phrase, "I've been damming the river," became a current by-word, as the usual explanation given that fall by unlucky miners for their season's failure. The "float" gold, as was ultimately found out, lodges on the riffles, or rapids, and not in the

THE "EMIGRANT'S" FIRST APPEARANCE
IN THE DIGGINGS.-1

deep holes, some hint of which I might have taken from my experience as a neophyte in wrestling with the pot-hole. In the gravel drift of the river-bars, the "pay-dirt" usually lay in "streaks" corresponding to the several strata as these had been successively super-posed one upon another.

The Indians were frequent visitors at the mining camps in this section. While the placers were plenty, shallow, and easily worked, they did a good deal of

1 Adapted from Mark Twain's "Roughing It," by permission of American Publishing Co., Hartford, Conn. See Appendix, p. iv.

spasmodic mining.   The pan and the wooden bowl—
the *batea* (bah-ta-a) of the Mexicans—were the implements they chiefly used for the purpose.   A half doz-
en or more of them would dig and wash diligently for
two to three hours, when they would hie themselves
off to the nearest store or trading-post to spend the

proceeds.   At
the "Mountain-
eer's Home," we
had a frequent
customer, who
pompously point-
ed to himself as
"me Jim, Akal-
de,"[1] and who
rarely missed an
opportunity to
impress upon us
the dignity of his
personage.   Jim
evinced a decid-
ed partiality for

"THE NOBLE SAVAGE."

bright calico shirts—at five dollars apiece; for which
he appropriated the bulk of the earnings of himself and
his handful of followers.   These shirts he would put
on, one after another, until he had perhaps a half doz-
en telescoped over his person at once, never taking the

1 Al-cal-de is the Spanish equivalent for Justice of the Peace; but under the
lax judicial methods of the Mexican regime, the functions and powers exercised
by the officials bearing this title were often little, if any, short of absolute.
Hence, to the unrefined Digger perception, as with Jim, alcalde came to be sy-
nonymous with "chief," or headman of the tribe or community.   For full history of this office see Shinn's "Mining Camps," New York, 1885.

trouble to remove or to cleanse the ones he had previ-
ously successively donned. Thus arrayed, he was fully satisfied to allow the rest of his august figure to remain exposed in its natural grace and symmetry. Occasionally, enough dust
would be dug out to lay
in a sack of flour, in which
case the lord would mount
the purchase—a hundred
pounds—on the back of his
spouse, and then stalk
along in her rear with true
savage self-complacency
as she trotted home with
the burden.

One day, the ordinary
routine of the Placerville
camp was broken by the
appearance on the street
of an elderly, lean, angu-
lar man, who from his
wagon proceeded to make
a speech and exhibit sev-
eral ugly gun-shot wounds
about the groin. He soon
drew a crowd around him.
It appeared, according to

MODERN DIGGER BELLE, IN CEREMONIAL
COSTUME. (FROM A PHOTOGRAPH.)

his story, that he had been a participant in the armed
collision which had taken place the day previous between the squatters and the anti-squatters at Sacramento, and in which several men had been killed and wound-

ed.   The speaker belonged, he said, to the squatters'
side, and had been attacked and driven off by an armed
posse, from whose vengeance he escaped only by plung-
ing into the American River and swimming across beyond their reach.   But he had not quit the field, he declared, without having given his assailants a valiant
fight; whereupon some one in the crowd sang out,
"What is your name?"   "My name is Allen," he responded.   "You must be some relation to old Ethan
Allen," another spectator suggested.   "Yes:" answered
the speaker, "I am a grand-son of the hero of Ticonder-
oga."   But, notwithstanding this avowal as to "the
great Jehovah" blood in his veins, he was, obviously,
still very much frightened.   He had traveled all night
to make sure of getting out of harm's way, and he now
appealed to his hearers to protect him.   At this, of
course, everybody present shouted, "We will, we
will!" and so the episode ended.[1]

Placerville was the first point in the mines reached
on the principal overland trail in the season of 1850,
and, early in July, the stream of emigrants from this
direction began to pour into the camp.   The first arrival was a party from my own town in Indiana—the
Fowler brothers—who had made the journey from the
Missouri River with an ox team in ninety days.   The
rush that season was very great, and soon every ave-
nue was filled with the new recruits.   A more disap-
pointed and disheartened lot of mortals than they were

1 This collision occurred on August 14, 1850, Charles Robinson, the squat-
ter leader, and later Governor of Kansas, being among the wounded.   The con-
tention between the squatters and the anti-squatters, which was a long and
serious element of disturbance in the State is treated of at considerable length
in Royce's "History of California."

could scarcely be imagined. They believed, as did many of the old-timers also, that the diggings had been worked out, and that the whole country had collapsed into utter ruin. The gloomy outlook was further aggravated by the prevalence of much sickness, which, at this camp, was owing largely to the stagnant, polluted water, which was mostly obtained from the abandoned prospect-holes, of which the streets were full. I was myself taken with typhoid fever several weeks prior to the first arrivals overland, and did not recover so as to be able to work till this camp

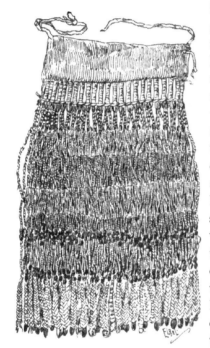

WOMAN'S CINCTURE. HOOPA INDIAN MAKE.—1

and the neighboring sections had become overcrowded with the newcomers. An ounce[2] a visit was the usual fee for medical attendance.

1 Reproduced by permission from Smithsonian Report for 1886, Part I.

2 The current trade value of gold dust up to September, 1848, was $12 per oz., at which date the merchants of San Francisco, in a public meeting, fixed the value at $16 per oz , and, though the actual average value, as determined by assays, was not far from $18 per oz. the rating established by the merchants was universally accepted as the standard while I was in California, and perhaps for years thereafter. See Hittell, "History of California."

In the latter part of August, Good arrived in Placerville from the Trinity diggings. He had come to
this congested labor market to employ men to work
for his firm—Brown, Pfouts & Co.—in that remote section, where the evil effects from the emigration had
not been, and were not likely to be, seriously felt. He
soon engaged about thirty men, at three dollars per
day and board. When we were going up the Sacramento Valley, the fall before, we met hundreds of men
coming from these same mines, cursing them as utterly worthless; yet, as a matter of fact, the yield here
was about as good as anywhere else in California.
And thus we found it everywhere—some coming, some
going; some praising, some damning.

Through Good's representations, I accompanied
him,[1] driving an ox team as far as Shasta, which was
the end of the wagon road in that direction, and
which was but a few miles from the scene of our first
mining exploitations. We had now to pack the rest
of the distance, some seventy miles, to the head of
the Big Canyon on the Trinity, where we proposed
to locate till the setting in of winter. Upon arriving
at our destination, I at once struck ounce diggings,
on a small sandy bar, near the river's edge; and one
afternoon I scooped up eighty dollars out of the water,
from the top of a bed of loose sand, inside of an abandoned coffer-dam. The gold was all fine scales, and
was obviously a quite recent deposit. Kendrick and
D. K. Wall bailed out the water while I did the wash-

1 The two Wall brothers, D K. and John D., of South Bend, Ind., and B. F.
Kendrick, of Rochester, Ind., were also of the party as traveling companions.

ing in a rocker, for which I paid each at the rate of ten dollars per day.

The Trinity abounded with salmon. Every morning there was a school of them inside the coffer-dam near by; and, with a few moments' work closing up the mouth of the dam with cobble stones, the fish were easily caught by the gills and tail, with the hand, as with their heads poked into the openings of the stones, they were wriggling to escape. I thus supplied myself with a superabundance of this "poor man's meat." On one occasion I saw a large specimen wriggling itself spasmodically to cross a riffle in the North Fork, where the water was scarce-

PROSPECTING IN THE TRINITY REGION.

ly deep enough to cover half its body. I crippled it with a stone, when it whirled over on its side and was floating away, as I caught it. Many were badly bruised from contact with the rocks when flinging themselves into the air in forcing the rapids. I saw one crazed in this way shoot across the river twice, the last time landing at nearly full length on the bank, where it was secured. Frequently, too, they were seen with one or more lamper ells clinging to their bodies. Indeed, so many perished in various ways that the Sacramento River, in 1849, was said actually to smell from the pollution.

In the course of a month or two, the approach of winter caused an almost total abandonment of the river. One day, I went down through the canyon to the Big Bar. This had been the largest mining camp on the river; but I now found it totally deserted. The utensils, implements, and camp debris of various sorts, not excepting bottles, were strewn about the brush shanties as if the occupants had decamped in a panic. Weaverville was the only camp west of the Coast Range that bore any semblance of a town, and to this point, as a winter quarters, flocked about everybody that intended to remain over winter in that region. I clung to my claim a fortnight or so, after the river below me had been wholly deserted, and when the nearest civilized habitation above me was six miles away, at Canyon Creek, where a sort of store was kept, and where, of Sundays, I obtained my week's supplies. On either side of the river, for practically an illimitable distance, the wild beasts and savages still held their pristine sway. It was a very imprudent thing for me to do; but there had been no trouble with the Indians up to that time, and I did not realize the danger to which I was exposed. The spot, too, was not at all a blithesome or an inspiring one; for all about me sharp, cragged mountains pressed one upon another, while immediately behind my little tent a sheer mountain wall, dark and frowning with its heavy growth of firs,

shut out the sun during all but about three hours of
the day.

I, at length, followed the crowd to Weaverville.
Here, about a mile from town, between Ten Cent
Gulch and East Weaver Creek, among the pines, I put
up for myself an eight-by-twelve log cabin, with shake
roof, and generous stick chimney.   The mountain lions
were very numerous in the vicinity, as their nightly
serenades kept me constantly reminded; but, with a

THE AUTHOR COMMUNES WITH SOLITUDE.

strong door securely pinned, I felt amply assured
against any undue intrusions on their part.   I did happen, however, on one occasion, to meet one of their
lordships on a trail in the thick chaparral, east of town.
I hardly need add that I was quite ready to yield him
the right of way, had he not, through his superior nim-
bleness, extended me that courtesy first. A young
man, who had come from my county in Indiana, but

whom I had never met there, came to my cabin here
sometime during the winter, claiming that he was not
able to support himself because of a crippled back.
He was a body-maker by trade, and was very glib in
recounting his travels and experiences, perhaps in contrast to my conscious rustic simplicity. I shared my
mite with him for six to eight months, and as a re-
ward he generously taught me to use tobacco. The
camp was by no means a live one; so that the breaking out of the Scott River excitement, toward the
close of winter, was
hailed as a timely
relief, and it precip-
itated a general
rush from Weaver-
ville thitherward.
Good happened to
be in Weaverville
with his pack-train
at the time, and
was employed to

HEAD OF A CALIFORNIA LION.—1

remove several stocks of goods from this point to
Scott's Bar, for which service he received a dollar per
pound, the distance being not far from a hundred miles.[2]

I did not join in the exodus, but early in the spring
returned to the Trinity, now locating on Reading's

1 Reproduced from Roosevelt's "The Wilderness Hunter," by permission of
G. P. Putnam's Sons, publishers, New York and London.

2 Good's firm also located on this bar where they kept a trading-post and
carried on mining, and where Good, in a letter, now before me, dated Sacramento, June 1, 1851, writes that he had the "biggest luck" mining he had had in
California. His partner, Joseph H. Brown, took out "near $5,000" in two
days, this including a nugget, "clear of quartz—nothing but virgin gold," and
"worth at $16 per oz, $3,140."

Bar, where I found the diggings pretty uniform and fairly good. One miner, a Missourian, assured me as to his claim here, that he "could make an ounce a day d——d easy by working d——d hard." Some claims paid much better than this, but the average per day to the man was perhaps not far from ten dollars. The pay-dirt was borne by hand to the river, where it was washed in cradles, or rockers. With the exception of one or two wheel-barrows, the Holland yoke, with buckets made of ten-gallon casks sawed in two, was the contrivance used for this purpose. This process was slow and laborious, and became more and more so as the claims were worked back from the water.

Besides, the carrying of the heavy buckets produced physical distortion, making one round-shouldered in a short time. In view of this unsatisfactory state of things, a party of us conceived the project of carrying the water to the dirt, instead of the dirt to the water, as was being done. A ditch from Weaver Creek to the bar would solve the problem. The idea was entirely feasible. The ditch need not be more than a mile or so long; the excavating could be done with the pick and shovel; the volume of water was more than ample; and as for head, it was only a question as to how far we should ascend the creek whether we should have barely enough or a thousand feet to spare. With this encouraging outlook, we began the work. The senior member undertook the part of engineer, and constructed what he called a "water-level" for the purpose. After a month or more of diligent toil with pick and shovel in the broiling sun, we turned in the water. What was our disappointment and chagrin upon this test to find that our ditch had been laid out wrong end first—that the mouth was about two feet higher than the head! A bountiful catch of the worthless lamper eel, coupled with an equally copious outpouring of irreverent interjections, was the sum total that the most of us realized out of the enterprise.

A Digger raid was the next notable event of the camp. All the horses of the vicinity, to the "unlucky" number of thirteen, were herded by two men at a stipulated price per head, and were carefully looked after during the day and closely corralled at night. The corral was situated just across the river, opposite the head of the bar. As a further precaution against the well-known partiality of the Diggers for equine feasts, the tent in which the men lodged was pitched immediately by the only entrance to the enclosure. Yet, in spite of all this care, the men awoke one luckless morning to find the bars let down and not a hoof in sight. The cause was at once divined—the Diggers had got in their work. A party from the bar were soon on the trail. The thieves, it was found, had set out with their booty to the eastward, but after awhile veered around to the westward. Whatever may have been the motive for taking this circuitous, out-of-the-way course, whether to divert suspicion from themselves at the expense of others of their kind, or to embarrass and elude pursuit, it was a ruse they had long

successfully practised.   In this instance, however, it
failed to subserve either of these purposes.   At a distance of about thirty miles by the route taken, over a
sinuous, wearisome mountain trail, the marauders were
completely surprised at their rancheria (ran-che-re-a)
and several of their number made to bite the dust.   A
deep, hidden ravine across their front partially foiled
a charge upon their position, and enabled the rest to
escape.   One horse only, and that the sorriest of the
lot, was recovered.   The sliced carcasses of the oth-

CALIFORNIA WOLF.—(REDRAWN FROM C. NAHL, IN "HUTCHINS' CALIFORNIA
MAGAZINE," 1858.)

ers were spread out upon poles to cure; for the wild
Digger of that day made no other use of the horse
than for food.   A hurried reconnoisance of the locality
disclosed signs of numerous abandoned rancherias, at
all of which fragments of horses and cattle were strewn
about, the latter attesting to the energy and persist-
ence with which the Diggers had carried on their depredations upon the whites, and that too (except in the
present instance) without detection or molestation in
any way.

VII.

DIGGER VENGEANCE—HUMBOLDT BAY.

ANOTHER collision of a somewhat more serious nature with the same band of savages, followed close upon the Hay Fork
affair, just detailed. The party, on their
return from the Digger horse-thief expedition, reported
that the section they had visited bore excellent auriferous indications, and that from appearances it had
never before been penetrated by the whites. Accordingly, a party of ten of us was at once made up to test
those indications; and, horses being now a rare com-
modity at the bar, we took the necessary traps together with five days' rations, upon our backs, and set out
in high spirits for the promised new El Dorado. Several of the former party were among our number, to
pilot the way, and of course to share in our expected
good fortune. Strangely enough, our only thought
was of diggings, not of Diggers. Two rifles, a shot-
gun, and perhaps a half dozen Allen "pepperboxes"[1]

1 Mark Twain thus not inaptly discourses of this make-believe weapon: "To
aim along the turning barrel and hit the thing aimed at was a feat which was
probably never done with an "Allen" in the world. . . . Sometimes all its
six barrels would go off at once, and then there was no safe place in all the region roundabout, except behind it. He might have added that "sometimes"
none of the "six barrels would go off at all."

comprised our equipment of weapons offensive and de-
fensive, all told.   We made our first camp where we
first struck the Hay Fork.   Our savory repast of
bread, bacon, and coffee was soon disposed of, when
each man rolled up in his blankets for the night, utterly oblivious as to any possible danger.   The next morning, bright and early, our frugal breakfast was over,
and we were pushing our way down the stream.   Presently, the site of the encounter with the Diggers a

few days
before was
pointed out
to us on the
opposite
side of the
river, all
now silent
and lifeless
as the grave.
But we still
took no fore-
bodings
from the sit-

CALIFORNIA LYNX.—(REDRAWN FROM C. NAHL, IN "HUTCHINS'
CALIFORNIA MAGAZINE," 1859,

uation.   We were delighted with the prospect that
opened up before us.   The mountains swung away
from the stream to the right and in front, leaving a
space of several thousand acres intervening.   This
space was comparatively open and level, and was
carved into a series of gentle, grass-clad undulations,
which here and there sloped away into rich, alluvial
bottoms, and through which, at frequent intervals,

bright, sparkling rivulets came plashing down from
their mountain sources. The general surface was
sparsely dotted with low, heavy-topped oaks, while
the higher points were crowned with dark-green tufts
of firs and pines, the whole being bordered about by
sombrous, massive mountains, as if to complete the
picture. We had so long been cooped up in the narrow mountain confines that we now felt that we had
room to breathe full and free once more. Yet, withal,
how inscrutable seemed the order of Providence, that
the stolid, "untutored" Digger should until now alone
have been privileged to look upon this scene of prime-
val beauty, one of the masterpieces of the great Artist! Thus, ages upon ages,—

> "Summers and winters came and went,
> Bringing no change of scene;
> Unresting, unhasting, and unspent,
> Dwelt Nature here serene."

But we had little leisure for indulging in the æsthetic
or the sentimental, and were soon scattered out among
the gulches, intent upon the more prosaic business in
hand. I had wandered away from the rest of the party
perhaps a quarter of mile, when I was startled by an
unearthly noise bursting upon my ears. Glancing up,
my eyes fell upon a Digger in uncomfortable proximity to where I was standing, and a further glance beyond revealed a dark, swarming mass of redskins on
a mountain bench, not more than a half mile away.
Their wild, frenzied whoops, yells, and contortions left
no doubt as to their animus. I paused for no further
hints. On the contrary, never before in my life, did I
so thank my stars for suppleness of joint, lightness of

heel, and length of reach as I now did till I rejoined my companions. I found them hastily consulting as to what should be done. The unanimous voice was for attack, and we at once charged at double-quick upon the savages. They, with a like celerity, scampered up the mountain side. Pursuit, we thus saw, would

be futile. Nor would it be prudent to remain where we were. The position was disadvantageous and untenable. Moreover, the traditional predilection of the redskin for midnight scalps, roasts, and the like now flitted athwart our visions. We, therefore, decided to retrace our steps to a more secure position. But, on our facing about for this purpose, the Diggers faced about upon us.

WOMEN'S CAPS.—1 HOOPA MAKE.
(SEE NOTE, P. 70).

We now held another moment's consultation, the result being that we turned upon them; and again they fled as before. This sort of charging and counter-charging was repeated once or twice more, when we abandoned the child's play, and proceeded finally to

1 Drawn from specimens in a collection belonging to the author.

withdraw. In doing this, we turned the point of an open ridge that lay across our course. No sooner had we reached the opposite side of this than the Indians, emboldened by our retreat, swept across the bottom we had just vacated, and came stringing along the crest of the ridge upon our flank, now supplementing their demoniacal yells and gyrations with volley after volley of arrow-shots. But a vigorous use of our few pieces kept the pusillanimous horde well at bay. We had to cross several deep ravines, where, as a precaution against the savages descending upon us while we were thus disadvantaged, our party divided, one half in turn guarding on the bank while the other half made the passage. But presently an inward trend of the bluffs brought the enemy within effective arrow-range, when, for a moment there was warm work. The flying missiles fairly streaked the air. Zip! zip! zip! they stuck in the ground among us and about us, their feathered ends quivering in the air. In quick succession, a hat-brim was pierced, an arm grazed, a leg perforated, a foot wounded. We scarcely dared look up lest the face or an eye be struck. A squad of the Diggers were skulking along in our rear, to recover the spent arrows. These now likewise pressed close upon us, skipping from clump to clump of chapparal to cover their approach. Several of our men began to waver. One turned to fly; but "Kentuck's" rifle, coupled with a vigorous admonition, brought this delinquent back to his senses and into the ranks. We well knew what panic meant, and this nerved us for the worst. Fortunately, at this critical juncture, we

were just entering an open circular space, where the
distance from the bluffs assured us comparative safety.
Near the centre of this space, stood a large lone pine,
with wide-spreading and low-drooping branches. We
hastened to this cover, where we stationed out pickets,
and threw up around the tree a little earthwork, the
crown of which we stuck thickly with chapparal to
break or ward off arrow-shots. For we had not the
slightest doubt that we should be stormed that night,
if not before. This spot was, in fact, the very one we
had in mind when we began our retreat. It was well,
too, that this was so close at hand, for the man with
the dart in his foot declared upon reaching the place
that he could go no farther. When we began excavating, the Indians looked on for a few moments si-
lently and queeringly, as if wondering whether some
of our number had been killed and were being buried.
But, when our real purpose dawned upon them, they
broke forth with a vehemence greater, if possible, than
before, in a prolonged and frantic effort to frighten us
from our shelter. The squaws and children, from first
to last, seemed to outvie the bucks in their demon-like
performances. A pebble about the size of a hen's egg
struck the ground with a thud near where one of the
men was shoveling. It must have been hurled with a
sling from the bluffs, a distance of more than three
hundred yards. These wild, furious demonstrations
to dislodge us were repeated a number of times during the afternoon, but with gradual abatement of energy and frequency, till near sunset, when the savages
broke out afresh in a prolonged and terrific pandemon-

ium of their whoops and fantastic pranks. But, still failing of their end, they, to our great surprise and relief, now one by one filed over the hills from view, and we saw them no more. At nightfall, one of our men, "Missouri Jim," volunteered to try to make his way to the bar for aid. It was certainly no trifling task—the running of that lonely twenty-five-mile gantlet, infested as it was by wild beasts and hostile savages. But "Jim"—a Wisconsin boy, by the way— was equal to the emergency; and the next afternoon a ringing shout went up from our little breastwork, as we espied about sixty of our friends with several horses file toward us through the gap of the divide. The country was now scoured for Diggers; but, aside from a superannuated squaw with a basketful of arrow-points, not a Digger appeared to view. Our little earthwork was thenceforward remembered as "Fort Necessity."[1]

The distance between us and the Indians when they did their most effective work was stepped the next day, and found to be two hundred and fifty paces. The arrows were elevated and discharged from a position considerably above us, which partly accounts for their long range. The leg-wound was mine. The outer and feathered end of the arrow was quivering with a sort of rotary motion when I first observed it, and I instantly whisked it out, casting it away at the same time. The arrow was driven with such force as to cut through and through, perforating the pants-leg and

---

[1] D. K. Wall, of Denver, Col.; A. B. Liles, of Roswell, N. Mexico; J. N. Laughlin and W. S. Robinson, of Humboldt County, Cal., are the only survivors of this relief party at present known to me.

"FORT NECESSITY."

the high boot-leg twice.

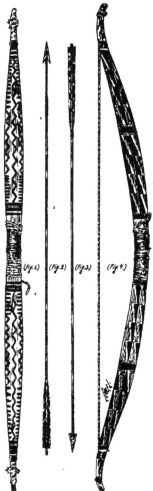

In the other case, the arrow entered the foot just below the ankle, through the eye-seam of the hard, heavy grain-tanned boot, and followed around the bone of the foot till the point struck the boot-sole on the opposite side, the body of the dart lodging among the delicate muscles of the bottom of the foot. The arrow-head was glass, and made a painful wound. We tried to extract it, but our butcher-knives had so long been strangers to the grindstone that the operation had to be deferred for more skilled hands and better instruments, both of which awaited us at the bar.[1]

(Fig. 1) (Fig. 2) (Fig. 3) (Fig. 4)

DIGGER BOWS AND ARROWS.–2

1 This man, one Willard, from Ohio, never fully recovered from his wound; but, regaining the use of himself sufficiently, he engaged in packing supplies for the miners along the Trinity. Finally, however, he was missed, and search being made, his remains were found up in a dark ravine, where the Indians had murdered him, and stripped and horribly mutilated his body.

2 Drawn from the originals in a collection in my possession. Fig. 1 and Fig. 2 are of the Modoc make, and were presented to me by George Graham, Eureka, Cal., who assured me that they were captured from "Captain Jack" and his band on the Lava Beds, at the time General Canby

I remained on the Trinity till sometime in September, when a recruiting officer appeared along the river enlisting volunteers for service against the Indians, under a call issued by the Governor. The miners of that region had acquired no very warm attachment for either the Diggers or the diggings; so that most of them were ripe for anything that promised a change. The inducement now offered was six dollars per day, the recruit to furnish his horse. About sixty men on the Trinity, myself included, responded to the call; and, bidding a not over tearful adieu to the "dear, damned, distracted" diggings, we set out upon the extremely rough trail across range after range of mountains for Uniontown, Humboldt Bay, the place of rendezvous, the distance being some ninety miles. An incident occurred on this trip that may be of some interest from an ethnological point of view. The advance of our party, as we were strung along the trail, captured a young Indian woman. When I came up she was sitting on the ground beside the trail among a group of our men. She was evidently badly frightened. Looking up piteously into the faces of the brusque men about her, she milked from one of her breasts, thus

was killed. Fig. 2 and Fig. 3 are of the Hoopa make. One of the arrow-heads is of copper and the other of flint. The bows are of yew wood, the backs of which (as of all of the Digger type) are "covered with a lining of sinew so carefully put on as to mimic the bark of wood, its thickness exactly fitted to the exigencies of the work to be done." Several kinds of stone, together with bottle-glass and (later) iron, steel and copper, were used for arrow-heads; and the arrow-shafts are usually in two parts, that to which the point is attached being about four inches long. This make of bow and arrow is probably the best and most artistic known. Fremont, in his "Memoirs," speaking of the metal-pointed arrows, says: "they could be driven to the depth of about six inches into a pine tree" Captain John G. Bourke makes substantially the same assertion. See Smithsonian Reports, Part I, 1886, and also same document for 1893, for a full description of these weapons and the method of their manufacture.

indicating that she had a babe dependent upon her, and appealing, it would seem, to our humane instincts, a quality of which the savage is credited with pos sessing very little, if any.   Of course, she was allowed to go her way, unmolested. We carried no provisions, as we counted on supplying ourselves en route with abundance of game. Our rations turned out to be very short; for all that we killed was one deer, and that not until the last day late in the afternoon.   Nor did we find things altogether to our liking after our arrival. The officer assigned to the command—Colonel J. H. Harper—was at the time engaged in a contest with the late General James W. Denver for a seat in the State Senate, and the canvass so engrossed his attention that he wholly neglected his military engagements. The re-sult was, that, after remaining in camp several weeks, with no prospect of being enrolled, we disbanded, but not without visiting a profusion of epithets more vigor-ous than polite upon the head of the aforesaid Colonel.

I remained at Uniontown (now Arcata) that winter. This point was then a commercial center of considera-ble importance, being a seaport, and as such the seat of a quite heavy traffic with the outlying mines. The sawmill had not yet been introduced in that section, and the frow and the whipsaw did duty as a substitute, the frow doing the major share of the work. The town lay immediately at the edge of the great red-wood forests, and the timber yielded so readily to the frow that the building material was chiefly manufac-tured in this way.   I was occupied during most of the winter getting out siding, for which I received ten

Seth Kinman

[Kinman was a noted pioneer and hunter of Humboldt Bay. He was a native Pennsylvanian, and when (Buch)anan was elected President he conceived the idea of making for that "public functionary" a (buck)horn chair When Kinman, as he here appears, arrived at Washington with his novelty, he was so greatly lionized that he followed up the experiment upon the incoming of every succeeding President down to Garfield, whose early assassination prevented the delivery of the gift. He took much pride in showing the many flattering notices he had received from the press. In 1884, when I last saw him, he was keeping at the stage station on Table Bluff a sort of frontier curiosity snop, where he served a limited assortment of "tangle-leg" to the thirsty wayfaring callers. Among his curiosities, was a fiddle he had constructed in part from the forehead of his favorite mule, whose spirit he hoped to meet in the Beyond.]

cents apiece. I made about a hundred pieces a day, after the timber was bolted. The axe, cross-cut, frow, draw-knife, and jack-plane constituted my kit of tools for this purpose.

The monotony of the winter was broken by a big fright from apprehended Indian hostilities. Two white men had been murdered on Eel River, presumably by the Indians. The deed and its supposed portent became a subject of much public concern, and soon grew into a general apprehension that the Indians designed to wage a war of extermination upon the whites. Public meetings were held nightly to discuss the situation and to arrange for defense. It was proposed to erect a stockade in the centre of the plaza for the safety of the women and children of nights and as a fortification in case of an attack. In the midst of the panic, a canoe containing several Indians was seen crossing the bay toward the peninsula. This incident was at once accepted as conclusive evidence that the Indians were collecting in that quarter preparatory to their general onslaught upon the settlers. That design, it was determined, should not be permitted to mature; it must be nipped in the bud. Accordingly, a whale-boat was brought into requisition; and a party of a dozen or so of us, armed to the teeth, headed, with muffled oars and under cover of night, for the supposed hostile camp. The landing was made and the rancheria surrounded before daylight, without our being discovered. One "Captain" Smith, an old, ponderous rustic, a typical "Kaintuck," was our commander, and he proved himself to know about as much of military tactics as a Digger would know of belles-lettres. Before it was fairly dawn we were ordered to fire upon the miserable shacks. The surprise was complete, and as quickly as the affrighted Diggers could crawl out they scampered for the nearest brush. Several of them were shot down as they ran. One big buck was perforated with sixteen bullets. The women now set up a long heart-rend- ing moan. The Indians were utterly defenseless; but their pitiable plight did not in the least restrain our valor- ous men from rush- ing down on the huts, plundering them of everything that was deemed of any value, and then putting the rest to the torch. In ran- sacking the lodges, a half-grown boy was found hidden away, and was dragged out. The little fellow begged piteously for his life; but he was coolly shot down, notwithstanding. It turned out ulti- mately that these Indians had no thought of attack- ing the whites; that they had no connec- tion with the Eel River murders; and that the scare over the anticipat- ed war of extermi-

KI-WE-LAT-TAH, OR "COONSKIN."-1

nation was based upon the veriest moonshine. The savages themselves, it may be added, could scarcely

1 Redrawn from a photograph of a life-size painting owned by the late L. K. Vood, at Arcata, Cal. Ki-we-lat-tah was a noted chief of the Humboldt Bay Indians, whose massive and dignified figure I saw many times, and who was one of the very few of his race that commanded the general respect and confidence of the whites. I am indebted to David Wood (son) for the photograph used.

have exhibited a more fiendish relish for rapine and
for blood than did the most of our men on this occasion.   I have ever since congratulated myself that upon seeing the defenseless condition of the Indians, I
had not the heart to join in this wanton destruction of
life and property.

Humboldt Bay was discovered by a party of wan-

HEAD OF A GRIZZLY.-1   (SEE APPENDIX, P. XI.)

dering miners from the Trinity on December 20, 1849,
and the first vessel that plowed its waters made its entrance on April 6, 1850.   This craft was the "Laura
Virginia," commanded by Lieutenant Douglass Ott-
inger, of the United States Marines.   It lies, by sea,
two hundred and eighteen miles north of San Francisco; is the best harbor between San Francisco and

1 Reproduced from Roosevelt's "The Wilderness Hunter," by permission of
G. P. Putnam's Sons, publishers, New York and London.

the Columbia River; and is the principal outlet of the great redwood region, which is the finest forest in the world. The port was at first prized chiefly because of its eligible situation as a supply-point for the mines of Northwestern California; but the fine bodies of ara- ble lands about the bay and in the neighboring Eel River Valley were rapidly settled up and converted into farms. In the spring of 1852, the lumber indus- try began to be rapidly developed, no less than seven sawmills, several of them of large capacity, being put in full operation within a year. Eureka was the prin- cipal seat of this activity, as it has continued to be down to this day. The town grew with correspond- ing rapidity; many vessels came and went; the mills buzzed away day and night; and the woods there- abouts resounded with the axe and the "Whoa, hush!"[1] of the logger. Everybody was busy; everybody had money;[2] everybody seemed contented and happy. Ev- ery logger owned his own timber claim and his own outfit, and thus exemplified the ideal condition that we are wont to assign to the ideal tiller of the soil. Those that worked for wages, as a large proportion in every civilized community always must, received for ordi- nary labor from a hundred to a hundred and fifty dol- lars per month and found. The big trees were not utilized in that primitive era. Three to four yoke of

1 The constantly recurring exclamation of the "Down-East" and the "Blue- Nose" (New Brunswick) ox-teamsters.

2 As a straw indicative of the prevailing flush times it may be mentioned that Seth Kinman, the noted hunter and antler chair-maker, and myself were ten- dered fifty dollars each to preside as the *orchestra* for a Christmas ball at Un- iontown, in 1852. Kinman's repertoire consisted mainly of an alternation of "The Arkansaw Traveler" and "Hell on the Wabash," and mine was little more varied or pretentious. He responded. My conscience had not yet reached that degree of elasticity.

PRIMITIVE LOGGING SCENE AT HUMBOLDT.

oxen with the two-wheeled trucks sufficed to convey the logs to the tide-water sloughs, whence they were rafted to the different mills.   Leeper, Liles & Company were credited with having cut and delivered the largest log that up to 1854 had been sawed at any mill on the bay.   This was a redwood, fifty-two inches thick at the top end and thirty feet long; and this was sawed by Joseph Bean at the Martin White mill. There was then little demand for redwood lumber in the San Francisco market, the spruce and Oregon pine being chiefly in request.   Logs at the mills commanded twelve dollars per thousand feet and lumber forty to fifty dollars.   But forty years have wrought a wonderful change in the methods and the demands of this industry at Humboldt Bay.   Redwood lumber is now the sort chiefly in demand, and no tree is so large as to be spared by the logger.   The simple primitive trucks had long ago to be cast aside.   The twelve-foot cross-cut saw, the donkey engine, a network of rolling-tackle, the skidded roadway, and a team of ten horses or twelve oxen constitute in part the elaborate and powerful appliances at present required.   In another particular the change is also conspicuous.   The timber lands are now mostly owned in large bodies, and the small independent logger with his own team and his own claim exists only as a pleasing memory. .

The native pastures in this section of the State, especially in the Bald Hills back of the redwood belt, were remarkably fine, and, consequently, game, particularly bear, deer, and elk, ranged here in great abundance. Until 1853, the citizens depended wholly upon the

hunters for fresh meat, that of the elk being the sort
commonly supplied. Joseph Russ and M. Barry
Adams—both lately deceased—were the first to open
a meat market. That was in Eureka, in 1853. Barry
presided at the block, and kept everybody about town
in good humor with his ever-ready fund of Celtic wit.
At about the same time, D. D. Williams and myself
introduced the pioneer milk ranch on the bay. We
had thirteen milch cows, for which we paid three hundred dollars apiece. Fresh milk sold readily at a dollar and a half per gallon, and fresh butter at a dollar
per pound.

In 1853, the Government established a military
post—Fort Humboldt—on the bay, of which Brevet
Lieutenant-Colonel R. C. Buchanan was the commanding officer, and which was garrisoned by two compa-
nies of the Fourth United States Infantry. Several
officers of the command rose to distinction in the late
Civil War, among whom were Generals Grant and
Crook, the latter the renowned Indian fighter. Grant
was then a Brevet Captain and Crook a Lieutenant
fresh from West Point. Of course, no one at that
day dreamed of the latent potentialities of these subse-
quently great Captains. Grant was a quiet, reserved,
unostentatious sort of man, whom nobody seemed to
know any further than that he was "Captain Grant."
He would sit on a store-box in Eureka alone for hours,
attracting little more attention than if he had been a
dummy.

The redwood forests have been incidentally noticed.
These forests, over five hundred thousand acres of

which lie in Humboldt County, are of so much Importance to Humboldt Bay, to Northwestern California, to the domestic improvement and the foreign com-
merce of the Pacific Coast, as to merit separate and
special mention. It is well known that the species
(*sequoia sempervirens*) is found nowhere else than on
the coast-belt of the north half of California. The
appearance of these phenomena and the impression
they produce upon the visitor have been thus aptly
portrayed: "There are not, I think, more impressive
forests in the world. The land is actually darkened
with them. You walk in some of them on a bright,
sunshiny day as you might in the gloom and darkness
of Alaskan forests. The impression that the atmosphere above is draped in fog, or is overspread with
the cloud-darkness preceding rain, is constant, except
where an occasional opening allows the sun to break
through. Nowhere in our forests is sunshine more ac-
ceptable or beautiful. It comes in long, yellow splint-
ers, or open, clear bars, lighting up the dead-gray bark
of the redwoods, the luminated cork-like bark of the
pines, and showering ineffable beauty on the clear
green undergrowth, particularly on the fleur-de-lis-
shaped circles of immense ferns which everywhere in
the shade cover the ground. The effect of this coming out into a break of sunshine from the gloom of the
forests, is very peculiar. It seems out of place in its
suddenness—as if one were instantaneously to emerge
from the darkness and gloom of rain into clear sunshine. Not a sound of bird, beast, or wind disturbs
the silence, and even the most of the streams steal

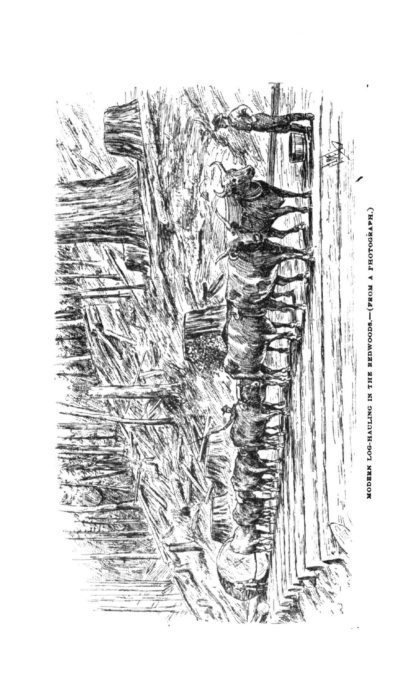

MODERN LOG-HAULING IN THE REDWOODS.—(FROM A PHOTOGRAPH.)

quietly seaward. It is a place where silence itself might feel the need of going on tip-toe. Fancy going mile after mile through trees one hundred and fifty to three hundred feet high packed as closely, one some-times thinks, as trees can conveniently stand, and breathe—where deep shade prevails, and where no noise, not even a leafy rustle or tree-shaken whisper is heard—and it can be imagined how different the feel-ing is than when in open ground and in full sunshine. After walking for half an hour thus, to have a break of sunshine slant in with its yellow light and color il-lumination, the invariable feeling is that the sun is bending to send in a salutation of light, peace and glory. But the size of these redwood trees, their num-ber, their grandeur, their immovably rooted bases, their beauty, their litheness, their remarkable straightness—none, nor all of these are anything like so impressive as their age. · They are nine hundred to fifteen hun-dred years old. Here are trees standing, not in ruins, nor even in the senility, loss of strength and color of age, but with intense exhibition of almost immortal strength, spanning and bridging past centuries. Holy men of old walked, it is said, with God; these trees have stood with and worshipped before him, while al-most countless generations have come, gone, and passed away. Age and strength, age and beauty, age and straightness, age and flexibility, here stand hand in hand, harmonizing the apparently irreconcilable, mak-ing apparent impossibilities possible and natural. Think of single trees yielding fifty thousand feet of redwood, and single acres of land yielding one million feet of lumber. Indeed, in a radius of one hundred and fifty feet, we in one place counted sixty trees, some of them three hundred feet high, and with a circumference of sixty feet two or three feet from the ground. All of the trees there are large. The acre of land on which those trees stood would yield much more than one million feet of lumber, or say enough to load four of the largest three-masted schooners. The size, quality, and grandeur of the redwood trees of California, and the extent of the redwood forests, have been the theme of many writers, and the admiration and wonder of the lovers of nature, until their fame is worldwide. But a slight conception can be had of their size and height until they are seen. All accounts seem fabulous until one stands amidst a forest of these monsters; stands at the base of a tree sixteen feet in diameter and four hundred feet in height, straight as an arrow, covered with massive layers of bark twelve to twenty inches thick." The first time I looked upon these wonders was when journeying from the Trinity River to Humboldt Bay. When I came down among them, I was actually spellbound, as I gazed upon their huge, shapely columns planted thickly about me and seemingly shooting up to the very skies. Of course, though their life is reckoned by the roll of centuries, yet they have their appointed cycle of years; and it is truly sad to contemplate their majestic forms, older possibly than the Sermon on the Mount, lying prostrate upon mother earth. Some of these have trees larger than a man's body perched upon their trunks; growths whose root-fibres have found sustenance in the immense bark,

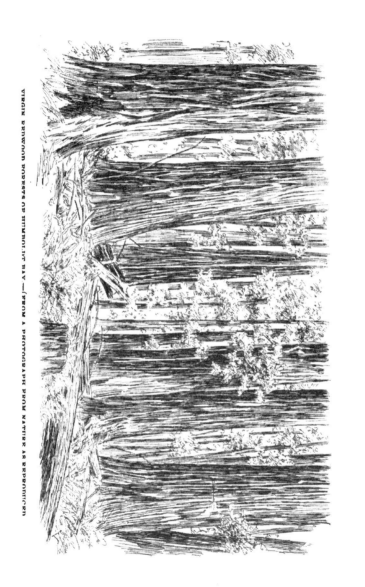

VIRGIN REDWOOD FOREST OF HUMBOLT BAY.—(FROM A PHOTOGRAPH FROM NATURE AS REPRODUCED UROPNOGEN)

and thus worked their way down into the soil. These giants seem to lose their footing more frequently after the close of a storm than during its progress. Our logging cabin was located in the midst of a section of these forests, and I often, at such times, lay in my bunk of nights, as here and there one after another of these mighty chiefs of the forest lost their hold and came tumbling to the earth, resounding as if each had brought down with it the thunders of heaven in its death-agonies. A section of one was cut at Humboldt Bay, twenty-five feet in diameter, to be exhibited at the Crystal Palace Exposition, New York, in 1854; but no vessel that entered the bay had the space to receive it, so that it was not shipped. This section was solid except a space of about a foot in diameter in the centre. Another, thirty-three feet through, stood on the pack-trail between the bay and the Klamath River. This was hollow and was used by packers as camping quarters.

In April, 1854, I took passage on the schooner "Sierra Nevada" for San Francisco; and, on May 16th, I sailed for New York, via the Nicaragua route, taking the steamer "Brother Jonathan" on the Pacific side, and the steamer "Star of the West" on the Atlantic side. Both vessels became historic afterward. The one was lost on the Oregon coast with all on board, and the other ran the gantlet of the Confederate guns in Charleston harbor, when sent by the Government to relieve Fort Sumter at the outbreak of the Rebellion. The voyage could scarcely have been more pleasant—fine weather, no accidents, no sickness, no deaths, good fare, accommodating officers, and agreeable passengers.   Distance from San Francisco, five thousand five hundred miles; time, twenty-three days; making, altogether, a journey of over ten thousand miles and an experience of five years and four months.

I may now be permitted a few concluding reflections.   The subjects of this narrative—the California Argonauts—present a truly interesting spectacle in history.   In 1849, forty-two thousand of their number reached the gold fields by land and thirty-five thousand by sea.   In 1850, the rush hither was still greater, and the stream continued to flow in year after year with little abatement.   From a population of perhaps thirty-five thousand before this tide set in, the number within four years swelled to three hundred thousand; and within the same period more than two hundred and sixty million dollars of gold was dug from the mines.   This tide of humanity rushing hitherward and overrunning those mountain wilds can be likened only to those mighty race-waves that in ancient times swept over from beyond the Euxine and overran the Continent of Europe.   In the present instance, nearly every race and clime of the globe was represented; yet the sturdy American type dominated all others, and impressed its character and its institutions upon the land.   These Argonauts were for the most part under middle-age, and the degree of pluck and energy they displayed in this novel field has probably never been paralleled.   They explored difficult and dangerous mountain recesses; upturned gulches and canyons; washed away flats and bars; turned rivers from their beds; tunneled mountains; sluiced away hundreds of miles of earth; built up towns and cities; developed agriculture; established courts of justice; set up and put in motion a state government wholly within themselves; and, in a word, gave an impetus to human progress throughout the globe to an extent never before equalled in the same period of time since the dawn of human history.

The Golden State itself is truly a unique land with a unique history. Widely isolated as it is betwixt desert and ocean from the great hives of humanity, it is a world of itself, and has built up a civilization in large measure peculiarly its own:

> "With high face held to her ultimate star,
> With swift feet set to her mountains of gold,
> This new-built world, where the wonders are,
> She has built new ways from the ways of old."

Yet it is not a world without its drawbacks. To me, surely, it did not afford an unceasing round of pleasure. Still, to me, as to most others that have once known and felt its peculiar fascinations, its mountains and valleys, its forests and streams, its fruits and flowers, its scenes and associations, are instinct with a romance, a charm, an indescribable something, that lingers in the memory like a fairy dream, and which time, nor distance, nor aught else, can ever lessen or efface.

APPENDIX.

MY PLAINS COMPANIONS.—Donahue I have never seen or heard
of since we separated on the plains. Good died of blood poison on
Carson River in 1853, when on his second trip across the plains to
California. Earl and Neal never returned to the States. Earl still
resides in California, where he married and has reared a large family. Neal died in 1883 at Shasta, near the scene of our first mining
experiences. Rockhill has from the first been following the for-
tunes of a mining life, and like most men in that calling has done
much rambling, being familiar with about every important mining
camp in the Rocky Mountains and beyond. He has been a resident
of White Pine County, Nevada, for nearly thirty years, and has
served that constituency acceptably in both branches of the Legis-
lature.

POSTAL FACILITIES —I received my first letter from home at
Reading's Bar, on the Trinity, after an absence of two and a half
years It cost me two and a half dollars, and I considered it very
cheap at that. Our nearest post office was at Sacramento. The
method of obtaining mail from there was by private enterprise, and
was without pretense of system or regularity. Some man would occasionally, as caprice happened to move him, procure a list of the
names of persons at a certain camp or camps and make the trip to
Sacramento, upon the stipulation that he receive a certain stated
fee for each mail package delivered, two to three dollars being the
usual charge.

A FLORAL PARADISE.—A local authority [Hittell, "History of Cal-
fornia,"] thus speaks of this striking feature of a California landscape: "There are grasses of various kinds and flowers in almost
unlimited number, including the golden poppies, buttercups, mal-
lows, pinks, nemophilas, roses, violets, larkspurs, and lilies without
end. The grass starts and the hills and valleys grow green, soon
after the first rains, in November and December; in February and
March the flowers commence; at one time the prevailing hue is
golden, at another yellow, at another blue, and at another purple,
according to the predominance of the blooms, and one tint or ano-

ther or a variety covers the plains and clothes the hills to their very summits." I chanced to be favored with an opportunity for observing this feature when probably at its best. It was in April, 1850, in the rolling oak openings westward of Hangtown, where I had gone in search of a horse that my partner and I had turned out to graze. The unusually copious rains of the preceding winter had been exceedingly favorable for the growth of herbage; and the section, being especially adapted for the purpose, now presented the aspect of a continuous meadow richly adorned with many species of variously colored and brilliant flowers. The billowy sweep of the land; the scattering, orchard-like oaks; the genial sky; the wealth of waving grasses and flowers; the playing of perfume-laden zephyrs; the shadows of fleecy cloudlets chasing each other across the landscape—such was the prospect as I beheld it, which in charm and gorgeousness of effect surely no artistic creation could equal, much less excel.

DIGGERS HARVESTING FOOD.—Quite to the contrary from the foregoing was the further spectacle presented to my senses on the same occasion. My attention was attracted by a number of squaws and children in a gentle sag among the rank herbage, and on approaching them I found that each had the typical burden basket, and was busily engaged in harvesting their annual crop of worms. These worms were mounted on the stems of the herbage, and were large and plump, very much resembling the tobacco variety. The process of gathering was to pluck the delicate morsel with the fingers, take one end in the teeth, and strip out the insides, and repeat the process till a number were thus treated, when the bunch would be twisted into a sort of knot and cast into a basket. This product, I learned, was mixed with pulverized acorns, and used for food. It is to be observed in this connection that the Digger was necessarily more the creation of circumstances than his civilized brother. Knowing nothing of the arts of agriculture, and having little, if any, traffic outside of his tribe, he was compelled to draw his subsistence from such local bounties as nature supplies, whether good or bad, generous or otherwise. If his lot fell along the bays and inlets, his chief dependence was upon shell-fish; if along streams, upon the finny tribes; and if inland or upon the desert, anything obtainable, including the most loathsome insects and vermin.

CACHING GOLD DUST.—There were no vaults or even safes in the mining camps in those days, and the inconvenience, to say nothing of the insecurity, of lugging gold dust about on the person, induced the miners frequently to resort to the cache as the most available substitute for those conveniences. This practice led to many curious experiences. In one instance, two men were on their way from a mining camp to Sacramento, when at a certain point one of them stopped suddenly by a conspicuous tree near the road, which also had a conspicuous limb pointing toward the ground. The man began to excavate with his mining-knife at the spot indicated by the pointer, and drew out two junk-bottles full of gold. One day, two strangers called at the only cabin on Reading's Bar—a small, rude round-log structure, covered with hides. It had been abandoned by its original owner or owners, and after that had many temporary occupants in the constant shiftings incident to mining life. It was now occupied as a trading-post, and the strangers by permission proceeded to remove a little earth in one corner, under the rawhide bunk, and exhumed an oyster-can filled with gold dust. At another time, two men had started from the bar for the States, and had gone about thirty miles on their way, when it occurred to them that they had forgotten their gold-cache. Sometimes the cache could not be readily found, when much nerve-force and perspiration would be expended in the search. I acknowledge having had one such experience myself. In another instance, a man, one of our messmates, had buried his gold dust in a buckskin purse, which the squirrels dug out and dragged up the mountain side, strewing the contents along their trail for several hundred feet. Not more than half of the gold dust was recovered, while the purse itself was never found.

THREE-CARD MONTE.—The first I saw of this most artful device of all for baiting "suckers" was at Placerville in 1850, after the first arrivals from across the plains. One evening, I was a spectator at Cold Springs, a neighboring camp, when the game was being dealt. A big crowd were around the table, among whom were four brothers, home acquaintances of mine, who were noted for their close-fisted, scrimping habits. The dealer affected utter recklessness in flinging the cards, and it frequently appeared as if the "winning card" could be pointed out with absolute certainty. The four brothers eyed the process with the keenest interest. The junior, a lad well in his teens, was made the custodian of the company's purse, which contained several hundred dollars in gold dust. At a certain deal, when one of those seeming "dead-open-and-shuts" appeared, the lad, nudged by one of the older brothers, clapped the purse on the card. But the gambler, feigning surprise and embarrassment, brusquely pushed the purse away, at the same time averring that he took "no bets from old men, children, or fools." At this, an older brother interposed and assumed the responsibility. "Well, but I have two chances to win to your one," persisted the man with the cards. "And that's the wrong card anyway." This pretended reluctance to accept the wager had the desired effect, making the dupes only the more eager and confident. The upshot was: the lad was handed a pointed stick with which to turn the card over. So over it went, and away went the purse and all. The gambler drew in the spoil, and with the utmost nonchalance began throwing the cards for a fresh deal as if nothing had happened—"the queen, the queen; the queen's the winning card; bet your dust on the queen." This incident is related simply as an illustration of spectacles at the gaming-table that became so common as scarcely to excite remark.

LAX ELECTION METHODS.—I cast my first vote at Placerville, at the first election held in California after the division of the State into counties.[1] I lacked three years of the age required by the constitution; but this was accounted no bar at this precinct at this election, the board ruling that every one that had been able to make his way to the country and shift for himself after his arrival ought to be allowed to vote. There was a spirited contest waging · between Placerville and Coloma for the seat of justice,[2] and the uncharitably inclined might have suspicioned that this fact had something to do with determining the liberal views of the board. I voted also, and served as a clerk of the election board, the next year, at Reading's Bar, at the first election held in Trinity County.[3] The board here was sworn in by one Bradley, whose only qualification for administering an oath was that once upon a time he had been a Justice of the Peace in the State of Mississippi. Here, as at Placerville, the polls were thrown open wide to everybody. The county seat question was also in issue at this election, Weaverville and Eureka being the principal contestants. Weaverville gave the bar no attention, while a representative of Eureka, C. S. Ricks, appeared among us and arranged for the opening of a polling-place, the result being that Eureka was honored with nearly every vote of the precinct. One precinct, "Symmes' Hole," which returned a tally-sheet with seventy-five names, was proved to be an outright forgery; and, generally, so much irregularity appeared that a new election was ordered. The same disregard of formality obtained elsewhere in the State. Good avowed that on going down the Sacramento Valley on an election day with his pack-train, he and his men were solicited to vote and did vote at every precinct they came to.

A QUEER CONCEIT.—Local prejudice was a very conspicuous trait of the isolated communities of the gold regions, where the newcomers were regarded with about the same sort of irreverence as

1 Held on the first Monday in April, 1850.
2 Placerville won, the camp having meantime changed its name from Hangtown to the less suggestive and more euphoneous appellation adopted.
3 Held on the first Monday in June, 1851.

old Jack Tar accords the land-lubber. They were dubbed "emigrants" as a distinguishing mark from the older inhabitants who
assumed blue blood because of their prior occupancy. The knight
of the ante-gold period, he of the *sombrero*, huge spurs, *serape*, etc.,
looked with no less commisseration, if not disdain, upon the arrivals
of '49 than did these in turn upon the arrivals of '50. The prepos-
session was not confined merely to the Coast, but followed upon the
discovery and opening up of new camps everywhere. In later times,
"pilgrim," "tenderfoot," and "stinkfoot" were indifferently substi-
tuted for "emigrant" as epithets of derision, especially in the Rocky
Mountains, in the sixties, when the great tidal wave of veteran
gold-hunters swept over from the Coast and here dashed against an
equally formidable wave of "greenhorn" gold-hunters rushing hither from the States. Mark Twain, in his "Roughing It," has deline-
ated some of his initiatory observations and experiences in this
regard. After depicting how he had served as the butt of the street
gamin, the boot-black, the half-breed, the stage-driver, the "bull-
whacker," and other like choice spirits of the select for the con-
doneless offense of being an "emigrant," he is moved to expatiate
as follows: "Perhaps the reader has visited Utah, Nevada, or California, even in these latter days, and while communing with himself upon the sorrowful banishment of those countries from what
he considers 'the world,' he has had his wings clipped in finding
that *he* is the one to be pitied, and that there are entire popula-
tions around him ready and willing to do it for him—yea, who are
doing it complacently for him already, wherever he steps his foot.
Poor thing, they are making fun of his hat; and the cut of his New
York coat; and his conscientiousness about his grammar; and his
feeble profanity; and his consumingly ludicrous ignorance of ores,
shafts, tunnels, and other things which he never saw before, and
never felt enough interest in to read about. And all the time he
is thinking about what a sad fate it is to be exiled to that far country, that lonely land, the citizens around him are looking down upon
him with a blighting compassion because he is an 'emigrant' instead
of that proudest and blessedest creature that exists on all the face
of the earth, a FORTY-NINER." Of course, the advent of the railroad, that greatest of levelers, has done much toward softening
down and rooting out this inordinate conceit, a relic of the barbar-
ous ages.

LAW AND ORDER.—We have heard much of the pistol and the
bowie-knife in connection with the early mining camps. Those communities were certainly in a very chaotic state, and as the inhabitants were constantly changing, there were few of those restraints
operating that come of social stability and settled neighborship.

At first there was a total absence of technical law, and if there had been any such instrumentality there would have been no adequate machinery for its enforcement. Gambling was everywhere rife; the "social evil" was unrestrained and unblushing; and Sabbath desecration was well-nigh universal; yet, for all that, I doubt if men were ever anywhere more scrupulous in the meeting of their business obligations. The following instances may be cited as typical: C. M. Long, of the firm of Pickard & Long, general merchants, Eureka, California, informed me that during the several years that they had done business at that point, (and they were the principal merchants there,) they had credited everybody that had·asked for it, and that the total of their losses on this account was but eight dollars. On board the vessel from Eureka to San Francisco, when I was en route for the States, I loaned an acquaintance, an ex-sailor, a "slug."[1] On our arrival at San Francisco, he went his way and I went mine. But, in a day or two, he called and paid me. On the same trip, I loaned another friend, one McLane, a hundred dollars. I did not see him again after our arrival till the steamer on which I was to sail was about to swing out from the wharf, when he came panting from nervousness and exhaustion, and handed me the money, explaining that he had been thus delayed in making collections, and evincing the utmost concern as to his honor in the premises. That these men paid me was entirely optional and voluntary on their part. They had no place of permanent residence, and practically nothing but non-attachable personal effects. Moreover, each had good reason to believe that my departure, already fixed upon, would in effect liquidate the debt, and, as a matter of fact, I have never seen or heard of either of them since. Now as to felonies in any of the camps where I was located during the period that I personally knew them: I can recall but a single instance of larceny: that at Coloma, where the thief paid the penalty at the whipping-post, mention of which has been made on pages 94 and 95 of the text. And I knew of the commission of but one capital offense where whites only were concerned, and that was one of murder and robbery, at Eureka, in 1852. Two men were hanged for the crime, one of whom voluntarily made a clean breast of his guilt and implicated the other. They were both tried by a people's court, which, under the circumstances, was the only expedient practicable. The organization of this improvised tribunal, and the proceedure of the trial, were entered into with the utmost gravity and deliberation possible; but in spite of all precautions the excitement inseparable from such an event finally overcame the crowd, and the trial of the last of the

1 An octagonal fifty-dollar gold piece, minted by private enterprise, and quite current as money in those days.

accused, who stoutly protested his innocence, and against whom
there was no evidence except that of the self-convicted criminal,
degenerated into a shameful farce. That it did so, however, was,
I am convinced, the fault of the method and not of the intent, tem-
perament, or moral obliquity of the actors in the affair. The same
outcome might have happened anywhere, however laudable the intent; so that we here have a most forceful argument against resort-
ing to such means where it is possible for the law to pursue its regular course. Speaking generally, I must say that, during an experience of about ten years in California and Montana, when society
was in its most chaotic state, and the machinery of the law was well-
nigh wholly wanting, I never personally witnessed a shooting or a
stabbing affray. Nor did I ever go armed myself; and in going about
in those regions, whether by day or by night, I felt not a whit more
apprehensive as to my person or property than I would today at
high noon in the lobby of the Palmer House, in Chicago.

THE DIGGERS AND THE WHITES.—The Digger aptitude for thiev-
ing was proverbial. This aptitude, especially among the mountain
tribes, disclosed itself most in horse-stealing, in the pursuit of which
marked boldness and dexterity were displayed. One instance was
related where the lariat was cut and the horse taken when the
picket end of the line was lashed to the owner himself. Good tells,
in a letter now before me, how, on the Upper Sacramento River, in
1851, the Diggers ran off ten of his best pack-animals, seven of which
he was unable to recover, though he pursued the thieves some forty
miles, and several times had a brush with them. The robbing of
the corral on the Trinity has already been noticed. Edwin Bryant,
writing in 1847,[1] asserts, upon what he considered trustworthy authority, that within the twenty years previous, the Indians had
stolen from the settlements between Monterey and San Francisco,
a total of two hundred thousand horses, one half of which number
could be distinctly enumerated. Nearly all these horses, he adds,
were slaughtered and eaten, the mountain Indians, who chiefly did
the mischief, having become so habituated to horseflesh that it was
their principal means of subsistence. We learn on the same authority that the first Indian horse-thief known to that region, set
out on his predatory career from Santa Clara, in about 1827, and
that from this point and this source the evil spread north and south
as fast as the extension of the settlements made such depredations
possible. As to the taking of life, however, it may well be doubted
whether the Digger instinct was so inclined, when not actuated by
motives of cupidity or of revenge. Fremont had difficulty with the

---

1 See his "What I Saw in California," New York, 1848.

Indians near Klamath Lake, in 1846, being on one occasion surprised by them at night and a quarter of his force killed or wounded. But I heard of no troubles of this nature taking place anywhere in the country during the first three years succeeding the gold discovery. In the Sacramento Valley, in the central and southern mines, and at Humboldt Bay, (except in the single instance mentioned elsewhere) there was no trouble whatever and no apprehension of trouble as to Indian depredations, and the two races intermingled one with the other upon the best of terms. The Indians often came about our logging cabin, near Eureka, and sometimes a half dozen or more of them would bunk for the night upon the floor. It was astonishing to see how many of them could huddle under a single blanket. A number of the squaws became the wives of white men. But this friendly disposition on the part of the one race was not always reciprocated by the members of the other race. We have seen where, without a shadow of real provocation, a rancheria near Uniontown was attacked, destroyed, and a number of the occupants shot down. That the whites, in this instance, labored under a misapprehension, did not in the least atone to the sufferers for the mischief wrought. In another case, at Humboldt Bay, a large part of the lower lip and of the lower jaw of a middle-aged buck was shot off. The man who was currently understood to have committed the deed had no other pretext for so doing than that the Indians, at a point about a hundred and fifty miles away, had, some months before, killed his brother and run off a large band of cattle that belonged to the two. The surviving brother became so wrought up over this outrage that he vowed vengeance úpon every Digger he should meet, and this buck was thus made to suffer for something of which he most probably had never even heard. Again: a logger's cabin near Eureka was rifled of some bedding and other traps. Some of the stuff was found shortly afterward in possession of an Indian at a little rancheria in Eureka. A pistol-shot finished the Indian and the guilt was avenged. Nothing was done, or tried to be done, with the offending white men in either of these cases: But the crowning scene in the drama occurred one night in 1860, when an unknown party, evidently whites, attacked a rancheria on Indian Island, almost within a stone's throw of the business portion of the city of Eureka. Not a man, woman, or child, save two or three that fled, was spared. Knives and hatchets or axes were from appearances the instruments principally used. On the same night similar attacks were made at several other points on the bay. Altogether, the number slain on that fateful night—bucks, squaws, and children—did not fall much short of one hundred and fifty. Within a few days, and apparently as a part of the same preconcerted plot, several rancherias in other sections of the county were visited with similar summary treatment. In no case, apparently, was resistance offered or resistance possible. The victims were taken unawares, and the work was massacre, simple and complete. Again, the law and humanity went unvindicated.[1] The object, doubtlessly, was extermination, and the object was well-nigh accomplished. In revisiting that section in 1884, I saw no Indians about the bay, except at Arcata, where I did see a remnant of them, apparently several families, quartered in the hollow of a redwood stump, the internal capacity of which had been somewhat enlarged by the action of fire. I also saw a dozen or so of the race up in the Bald Hills, about fifty miles back from the bay. Born and grown up in this locality, they had been dispossessed of their lands by the Government, without compensation, and by order of the same authority removed to a reservation in another section. But, obviously, to the red man, no less than to the white,

"Dear is the shed to which his soul conforms,
And dear the hill that lifts him to the storm.
And as a child, when scaring sounds molest,
Clings close and closer to the mother's breast;
So the loud torrent and the whirlwind's roar,
But bind him to his native mountains more."

This fragment of the race would not remain on the reservation, but returned to their "native mountains." Here, they were now regarded as trespassers, and were compelled to pay for the little native pasture upon which their few ponies subsisted, while they themselves eked out an existence as best they could, chiefly by means of such odd jobs as the whites might see fit to give them. Several of the women were the deserted wives of white men, and were now struggling for a living for themselves and children by making baskets and other wicker work. So competent and trustworthy an authority as the late John Ross Brown, in speaking of the troubles by which the Indians of the Humboldt region became reduced to such an extremity, says: "I am satisfied, from an acquaintance of eleven years with the Indians, that, had the least care been taken of them, these disgraceful massacres would never have occurred. A more inoffensive and harmless race of beings does not exist on the face of the earth; but whenever they attempted to procure a subsistence they were hunted down; driven from the reservations from the instinct of self-preservation; shot down by the settlers upon the most frivolous pretexts; and abandoned to

1 The affair occupied the attention of the grand jury, which, after severely condemning the butchery, dismissed the case upon the alleged ground that no clue could be obtained as to the identity of the perpetrators. For further details of this atrocity see "History of Humboldt County," San Francisco, 1882.

their fate by the only power that could afford them protection."
The characterization, "inoffensive and harmless," can hardly be applied to the mountain tribes of Northeastern California, though
possibly it might in the first instance.

EARLY CALIFORNIA PRICES CURRENT.—Delano's "Life on the
Plains and at the Diggings," gives the following as the prices paid
at Lassen's Ranch, on September 17, 1849:

Flour, per 100 pounds ....$	50.00
Fresh beef, per 100 pounds..	35.00
Pork, " " "	75.00
Sugar, " " "	50.00
Cheese, per pound..	1.50

H. A. Harrison, in a letter to the "Baltimore Clipper," dated
San Francisco, February 3, 1849, gives the following price-list:

Beef, per quarter..	$20.00
Fresh Pork, per pound...	.25
Butter, per pound...	1.00
Cheese, per pound...	1.00
Ham, per pound..	1.00
Flour, per barrel..	18.00
Pork, per barrel.. ....$35 to	40.00
Coffee, per pound..	.16
Rice, per pound..	.10
Teas, per pound..60 cents to	1.00
Board, per week...	12.00
Labor, per day..$6 to	10.00
Wood, per cord..	20.00
Brick, per thousand...$50 to	80.00
Lumber, per thousand..	150.00

William D. Wilson, writing to the "St. Joseph Valley Register,"
on February 21, 1849, gives the following schedule of prices at Sutter's Fort:

Flour, per barrel..$ 30 to	$40.00
Salt Pork, per barrel...\. 110 to	150.00
Salt Beef, " .... 45 to	75.00
Molasses, " .... 30 to	40.00
Salt Salmon, " .... 40 to	50.00
Beans, per pound...	.20
Potatoes, "	.14
Coffee, " ....20 cents to '	.83
Sugar, " ....20 cents to	.30
Rice, " ....20 cents to	.30
Boots, per pair...$20 to	25.00
Shoes, " .... 3 to	12.00
Blankets, " .... 40 to	100 00

Transportation by river from San Francisco to Sacramento, he
says, was $6 per one hundred pounds.   From Sacramento to the mines
by team at the rate of $10 for every twenty-five miles.

John H. Miller, writing to the "St. Joseph Valley Register," October 6, 1849, gives the following prices at Weberville, 60 miles from Sacramento:

Wagons	$40 to $80 00
Oxen, per yoke	50 to 150.00
Mules, each....	90 to 150.00
Board, per meal, $1 50, or per week.............................	21.00
Beef, per pound... ....40 cents to	75
Salt Pork, per pound..40 cents to	.75
Flour, per pound..25 cents to	.30
Sugar, per pound...30 cents to	.50
Molasses, per gallon.............. .:................ ....$2 to	4.00
Mining Cradles.................................... ....$20 to	60.00
Mining Pans ....$4 to	8.00

[After the rainy season set in, the roads to the mines became extremely heavy, and the rate of transportation for the same distance during the most of the winter was $1 per pound, which on the average increased the prices here given more than 100 per cent.—AUTHOR.]

THE GRIZZLY BEAR.—This ponderous and redoubtable beast, perhaps the most formidable animal on the continent, figures with much prominence in early California. Its image was emblazoned on the flag under which the non-Spanish residents of that country first revolted against the Mexican rule, and today the same image occupies a place quiescently beside the traditional goddess on the chosen arms of the State. The grizzlies were very numerous on the Coast, even down to my time there, especially in the lower valleys in the season of berries. Their feats were a staple theme of the current every-day conversation. Along the Sacramento River, in the fall, wild grapes were abundant, which attracted many of the species from the mountains bordering the valley. As we were going up the river, in the fall of 1850, I inquired of a Missourian, who, with his wife, was keeping a sort of station by the roadside, whether there were many grizzlies thereabouts. "Oh, yes:" he ejaculated, "a right smart sprinkle of 'em." Then he went on to relate in his peculiar vernacular how, the night previous, one had come poking his nose under the edge of the tent where he and his wife were abed; how he had lighted a match to the bear's nose; and how the bear, at the smell of the sulphur, had scampered off in a fright. The grizzlies were also very plentiful about Humboldt Bay. The underbrush here was extraordinarily thick and tangled, and bore berries in great profusion and variety. In the proper season, the tops of these berry-bearing bushes were everywhere bent down or broken off by the grizzlies in their clawing after the fruit. During one summer, we were every morning regaled with the sight of the huge footprints of one of these monsters, where, the night before, he had deliberately waddled along on our cattle-trail, over which we were compelled to pass back and forth at least once every working day of the week. We did not put ourselves out of the way to seek a closer acquaintance with "Old Ephraim" himself. As a rule, he was given a wide berth, by professional hunters, as well as others. Once, a friend[1] and myself, in crossing over from Eel River to the bay, came upon five of the beasts on the trail a short distance ahead of us. When they espied us, several of them reared up on their haunches, "sized us up" a moment, and then, resuming their all-fours, they all contemptuously swaggered off about their business. We, with becoming grace, brooked the insult and allowed them to go their way. The grizzly was not considered dangerous, except when it was wounded or was come upon in close quarters unawares. Roosevelt, in his hunting-books, mentions several instances where, in the Rocky Mountains, men were killed at a blow of their paws; but, while I heard of a number of cases in California where persons were badly mutilated in their clutches, I never heard of a person there being killed by them outright. The worst case of mutilation that came to my knowledge was that of one L. K. Wood. This man was a member of a party that, in their wanderings in the fall of 1849, discovered Humboldt Bay, and they were in the mountains south of Eel River when the encounter took place.[2] With winter at hand, strength reduced, health impaired, provisions exhausted, and ammunition nearly run out, they were trying to work their way to the settlements, some three hundred miles away. The original party had disagreed and separated, the one to which Wood belonged now consisting of three men besides himself,—Thomas Sebring, Isaac Wilson, and David A. Buck. Entering a patch of mountain prairie, in the section mentioned, they came upon a group of eight grizzlies, and, though the men were so exhausted that they could hardly drag themselves along, yet they determined to attack the grim customers. When Wood was within about fifty steps, he leveled his rifle upon the one nearest him and fired. The bear tumbled over, biting and tearing the earth with all the fury of one struggling in the agony of death. Wilson, at the same time, dis-

---

1 This friend, whose name was Head, was, in one respect, peculiarly constituted. The mosquitoes in some places about the bay literally swarmed. I had my handkerchief bound about my head and neck, and was kept busy fighting the pests, notwithstanding; yet he strode along, evincing the utmost complacency, protesting that the ravenous tormentors passed him by without so much as thinking of molesting his person in anywise.

2 Wood wrote a graphic account of this affair in 1856, which was reproduced in the "History of Humboldt County," to which I am indebted for the details here given.

charged his rifle with telling effect, and now the two bears lay before them apparently dead. Five of the group retreated up the mountain, but one of those still unhurt cocked itself upon its haunches, seeming to deliberate as to the course it should pursue. Wilson sprang for a tree, seeing which the grizzly made a furious dash at Wood who was nearest it. But Wood also succeeded in reaching a small tree, a buckeye, where with clubbed rifle he beat off the attacks of the infuriated beast for a few moments. But now, to his utter astonishment, the bear that he supposed he had killed, sprang upon its feet and also came bounding toward him with all the ferocity that agony and revenge could arouse. The first spring the monster made upon the tree broke it down. Wood gained his feet and rushed to another small tree, about thirty paces away, the wounded bear grabbing at his heels at every bound. Grasping the sapling with one hand, he swung around it, thus clearing himself from the bear, whose momentum carried it headlong down the hill, some twenty paces beyond, before it could recover. Wood now, with all the energy of desperation, endeavored to scale the tree, but before he had ascended more than six feet the second bear came up, seized him by the right ankle, and dragged him to the ground. At about the same instant the wounded bear returned and caught him by the shoulder. The other still gripped his ankle, and now the two pulled apart, as if to tear their victim limb from limb. To use Wood's own words, "my clothes and their grip giving way occasionally, saved me. In this way they continued until they had stripped me of my clothes, except a part of my coat and shirt, dislocated my hip, and inflicted many flesh wounds—none of the latter, however, very serious. They seemed to be unwilling to take hold of my flesh; for, after they had torn the clothes off me, they both left me. The one went entirely away, and the other (the wounded one) walked slowly up the hill, about a hundred yards from me, then deliberately seated herself, and fastened her gaze upon me as I lay upon the ground perfectly still." But the first sign of life that came from Wood brought the bear back to him pell-mell, roaring at the heighth of her power at every jump. Now, poking her nose violently against his side, she "raised her head and gave vent to two of the most frightful, hideous, and unearthly yells ever heard by mortal man." But Wood remaining composed and perfectly still, the bear, after a few minutes, again left him, going about a hundred yards away, and setting back on her haunches, with eyes full aglare upon him. He managed, however, without a renewal of the attack, to drag himself back to the buckeye tree, where he had first sought refuge, and which, with much difficulty, he succeeded in climbing to a

point about eight feet from the ground.   Wilson, now observing
Wood up the tree, ventured toward him, whereupon the bear again
made a ferocious charge.   Wilson barely saved himself by spring-
ing up a tree near Wood as the bear lunged at him.   Now the bear
seated herself between the two men, keeping her eyes steadily upon
them, and savagely growling upon either of them making the
slightest stir.   Wood's gun was disabled, and, observing Wilson deliberately drawing a bead upon their implacable antagonist and
not pulling the trigger, he entreated him to "Shoot her! for God's
sake, shoot her! she is the one that caused me all my trouble."   But
Wilson replied, "No sir; let her go—let her go, if she will."   And
pretty soon she did disappear for good.   What Buck and Sebring
were doing while this exciting scene was enacting, Wood does not
say, perhaps feeling that since they failed to come to his relief, the
natural inferences were better left unsaid.   Wood came out of the
encounter so badly disabled that it became a serious question as to
what should be done in this extremity.   There was an Indian rancheria in the neighborhood, and the chief was besought to care for
him till his companions could make the settlements and return.
This dignitary consented, and, after taking as compensation all the
trinkets and other stuff the party could spare, even to Wood's
blankets, he turned upon his heels, walked away with the prize,
and was seen no more.   A consultation was now held, somewhat
aside from Wood, but in the course of which Wood heard Wilson
exclaim, "No, sir; I will not leave him! I will remain with him, if
it is alone: or I will pack him if he is able to bear the pain."   Wood's
dislocated leg had by this time become much swollen and inflamed,
and was so sensitive that he could scarcely bear to have it touched.
But these manly and heroic words of Wilson stirred the sufferer to
almost superhuman resolution.   The upshot was, that Wood was
lashed upon a mule, carried to the settlements, and his life saved.
I knew him well afterward.   He remained badly crippled all his
life, requiring the use of canes or crutches.   He was the first Clerk
of Humboldt County, where, near Arcata, he died a few years ago,
and where his children still occupy the old homestead.

LIST OF ST JOSEPH COUNTY ARGONAUTS.—I have prepared with
considerable care the following list of the names of residents of St.
Joseph County, Indiana, that crossed the plains to California in
1849.   I am indebted for much of the data of this list to contempo-
raneous files of the "St. Joseph Valley Register," which were kindly
placed at my disposal by Schuyler Colfax, of South Bend, Indiana.
Those printed in Roman (84) are dead; those in *italics* (22) are living;
those in SMALL CAPITALS (6) are missing.   In other words, about
three-fourths of this number are dead.   This ratio of the dead to

the living is probably not far from correct as applied to the whole of the emigration of that year; that is, of the seventy-seven thousand that entered the gold fields in 1849, nearly fifty-eight thousand today belong on the death-roll:

Allen, Abram ....Mishawaka
Armstrong, Simeon..   "
Bertholf, Abram B...   "
Black, Francis.......   "
Bratt, John...............Centre
Bertrand, Charles. ..South Bend
Busha, George......   "
Bronson, James C ....   "
Bressett, Lewis. ....   "
Baer, Adam.........   "
Crosby, Dr. A. B ....New Carlisle
Cutting, Dr.........   "
Chapman, Dr. Jared......Greene
Curtis, William...........Olive
Caldwell, Cassius ....South Bend
Carpenter, Ezra G...   "
Cottrell, Samuel L...   "
Coquillard, Jr., A....   "
Comparet, Louis G...   "
DE GROFF, G ....   "
Day, John..........   "
Doan, James...... ..   "
Donahue, Francis ....Centre
DONAHUE, MICHAEL......   "
Doolittle, James ....Mishawaka
Doolittle, Hull J......   "
Doolittle, George....   "
Eaton, James...............Olive
ESLINGER, MATTHIAS.. Madison
Earl, William L......South Bend
Fassett, Chauncey S..   "
Ford, Alex. J........Mishawaka
Farley, Joel...............Penn
Frazier, Alex. H..........Olive
Garwood, Sol..............   "
Garoutte, Jere. M....New Carlisle
Good, William S.........German
Gish, David E.......South Bend
Grossnical, Jacob....   "
Harris, Samuel.....   "

Horrell, Johnson.....South Bend
Horrell. James I.....   "
Henricks, Dr. John A.   "
Hopkins, Simeon W..   "
Hartwell, James ....Mishawaka
Harris, William......... .Harris
Johnson, John C.....New Carlisle
Johnson, Evan C.....South Bend
Johnson, Pierce N...South Bend
Johnson, Cyrenius....   "
Kinsey, Philip W....   "
Kelley, John............ .Centre
Kelley, Mrs. John. ....   "
LAMBING, FRED......South Bend
Lewis, Charles W....   "
Lindsey, Tipton......   "
Linderman, John.....   "
Leeper, David R .....   "
Labadie, Anthony...   "
Miller. William......   "
Miller, Matthew B...   "
Maslin, William. ...   "
McCoskry, David....   "
McNabb, Horton.....   "
McCOY, FELIX.......   "
Monson, Rev. W. C......Liberty
McCartney, Thomas ....German
McCartney, James.......   "
McCartney, Benj. F......   "
Miller, John N...........   "
McCullough, Wm. S......Greene
Merrifield, Geo C.....Mishawaka
Mathews, James ....   "
Metzger, Joseph E.......Harris
Norton, William. ...South Bend
Neal, Thomas Dudley.....Greene
Needham, John W...New Carlisle
Pierce, Charles......   "   "
Phillips, Melvin R..........Penn
Pierson, George......South Bend

Page, Francis.......South Bend
Rush, Hiram........   "
Rush, Mrs. H. (Sarah).   "
Rush, Miss Sarah.....   "
Rush, Miss Ellen.....   "
Reynolds, Ethan S....   "
Robinson, "Col." Abe B.   "
Rulo, William......   "
*Rockhill, Thomas........*Portage
Rush, D. Clinton....New Carlisle
Snyder, Joseph.... ......Harris
Sales. Jack and Boy..Mishawaka
Stocking, Walter V..   "
Shuffler, Reuben.... ......Olive
Spencer, Philo G..........   "
Stebbins, George ....   "

Snavely, William J..South Bend
Sherland, Luther....   "
Tutt, Charles M......   "
Trainor, Daniel......   "
Tingley, Simeon D.......Greene
Towner, —— ....Olive
Tibbetts, N. B.......Mishawaka
Vessey, John........South Bend
Woodward, J. E......   "
Whitman, William G.   "
White, Joseph.......   "
Woodward. William L.   "
Willoughby, Dr. D. W. C.   "
Wing, A. M..........Mishawaka
Wilson, Charles L....   "
Ward, Daniel..............Clay

ERRATA.

Page 75, line 2 below picture, for "log" read "adobe."
For "Donahue" read "Donighue."
For "Dr. A. B. Crosby" read "Dr. Averill *E*. Crosby."
For "John N. Miller" read "John *H*. Miller."
For "Col. Abe B. Robinson" read "Col. Abe *G*. Robinson."
Linderman, Lambing, and Eslinger are still living.
Towner, Stebbins, and DeGroff went from LaPorte county.

www.ingramcontent.com/pod-product-compliance
Lightning Source LLC
LaVergne TN
LVHW012202040326
832903LV00003B/74

ERRATA.

Page 75, line 2 below picture, for "log" read "adobe."
For "Donahue" read "Donighue."
For "Dr. A. B. Crosby" read "Dr. Averill *E*. Crosby."
For "John N. Miller" read "John *H*. Miller."
For "Col. Abe B. Robinson" read "Col. Abe *G*. Robinson."
Linderman, Lambing, and Eslinger are still living.
Towner, Stebbins, and DeGroff went from LaPorte county.